Life Is Like
Licking Honey
off a Thorn

Life Is Like
Licking Hney
off a Thrn

Reflections on Living Wisely
in this World of Pain and Joy

Susan Lenzkes

DISCOVERY HOUSE
PUBLISHERS®

Discovery House Publishers is affiliated with RBC Ministries, Grand Rapids, Michigan.

Requests for permission to quote from this book should be directed to: Permissions Department, Discovery House Publishers, P.O. Box 3566, Grand Rapids, MI 49501, or contact us by e-mail at permissionsdept@dhp.org.

Unless otherwise stated, all Scripture quotations are from the Holy Bible New International Version® (NIV®), © 1973, 1978, 1984 by Biblica, Inc.™ Used by permission of Zondervan. All rights reserved worldwide. www.zondervan.com. Other versions used: The Living Bible (TLB), © 1971. Used by permission of Tyndale House Publishers, Inc., Wheaton, IL 60189 USA. All rights reserved. The New King James Version (NKJV), © 1979, 1980, 1982 by Thomas Nelson, Inc. Used by permission. All rights reserved. The Message, © 1993, 1994, 1995, 1996. Used by permission of NavPress Publishing Group. New Revised Standard Version (NRSV), New Century Version (NCV).

Library of Congress Cataloging-in-Publication Data
Lenzkes, Susan L.
    Life is like licking honey off a thorn : reflections on living wisely in this world of pain and joy / from the heart of Susan Lenzkes.
        p. cm.
    ISBN 1-57293-069-1
1. Consolation. I. Title.
    BV4905.3 .L46 2002
    242—dc21   2002002082

Printed in the United States of America

Third printing in 2011

To
Dr. Dennis and Lynette Baker
and
Dr. Tom and Joan Correll

You willingly walked into our tangled briar patch
carrying buckets overflowing with
the healing honey of God's love.

First you, Tom, for six sacrificial months, then you,
Dennis, for an amazing two years and 65,000 miles of road!

Do you know how very *grateful* I am,
how eternally grateful our *entire congregation* is?
You lovingly tended us until we discovered that
these briar patches were meant to bear *fruit*!

We hope your buckets are filled with sweet berries.

You will always belong to us, you know,
no matter where you go. You are forever loved.

We thank and praise You, Lord Jesus, friend to sinners.
Above all, this book is dedicated to Your honor and glory.

Dearest Jesus,
You took our thorns.
You gave the sweet honey of
life in Your presence
that starts
right now
and
never ends!

Contents

Ackn*owle*dgments

I am grateful for . . .

The quote by novelist and journalist
Louis Adamic (1899–1951) that provided the title
"My grandfather always said that living is like licking honey off a thorn." What a vivid picture of living out God's joy in this often painful world.

My dear, dear sisters and brothers at
Discovery House Publishers
Talk about sweetness in the midst of life's pain. The honey of your patience has dripped for six long years as you've lovingly prayed and waited for me to write again, and then waited some more as the due date for my manuscript tip-toed by. I have asked God to reward you by touching the lives of thousands more through our ministry together as He strengthens and encourages hurting people and increases His glorious kingdom. To Him be all the glory!

My wonderful family and precious friends at
Vista Grande Church and beyond
This book is the product of the power of God in answer to your loving support and prayers. Some of you have been praying for a *long* time! And some of the content is the gift of your sweet presence in my life. Thank you hardly covers it. I thank God for you constantly comes closer.

Every person quoted in these pages
Especially Suzanne Sparks, who now expects royalties.

Friends and family who've read certain pages
and laughed and cried and said it's good
Herb always did that; you helped me not to miss him so much.

Julie Link, my wonderful editor,
who is not allowed to edit this acknowledgment
Your skills and encouragement are priceless. Besides, you're just
plain fun to work with. (Notice how I ended that sentence with
a preposition? Live with it!)

Introduction

EVEN with a wounded finger thrust into my mouth, I managed to mutter a complaint. Sure, it's a beautiful rose, but why the vicious thorns? Talk about spoiling a good thing."

It didn't matter that there was nobody to hear me. I was just getting started.

"And what about that bee chasing me? Can someone explain why bees—the very creatures that produce something as sweet as honey—threaten us with stingers?"

Perhaps because no one was around to respond to my peevishness, God showed some interest. Quietly, He planted a question or two of His own in my garden of gripes.

"Did you ever wonder why thorny stems are topped with gorgeous, fragrant flowers? Did you even think of asking why one of my stinging insects works constantly to make the sweetest nectar on earth? Need a hint? It has something to do with mercy and grace."

Oops. "I come to the garden alone, while the dew is still on the roses. And the voice I hear, falling on my ear, the Son of God discloses. And He walks with me, and He talks with me. And He tells me. . . ." Well, He tells me that I'm asking the wrong questions, for one thing. He tells me that I'm looking at things backwards.

Gently, He reminds me that every sweet thing still in this world is an undeserved gift of His grace and love. Every painful barb is here courtesy of humanity's own rebellious choice.

God knows full well, and I know too, why this world is full

of stabs and stings. God's own creation—the man and woman He created in His perfect image and to whom He gave the gift of free will—invited the thorns into God's flawless garden by choosing to believe the Evil One's lies rather than God's truth. We have been swallowing lies and making wrong choices ever after, proving ourselves to be their children.

Thus our world became a tangled briar-patch of sin that separated us from God . . . broke us at the core . . . infested our relationships . . . blighted God's beautiful creation . . . introduced us to death. Living became barbed and painful.

God was asking me to admit that my viewpoint should start from the perspective that pain was mankind's own choice, and then to look beyond that pain to His promised blessings and joy. He was asking me to realize that, were it not for His sweet grace, thorns and death would be—and, indeed, should be—all we get.

But God's holy justice is saturated in the honey of His mercy and compassion. He revealed a love that is almost beyond belief. The Rose of Sharon, God's Beloved Son, placed on His own head our thorny crown.

On my desk sits an actual crown of thorns that I borrowed from my friend Sandee Reynolds. As I finished writing this book about thorns, I wanted a constant reminder of what Jesus endured for us. The thorns sitting before me are long, sharp, and frightening to contemplate. Jesus wore such thorns so that you and I could have an eternity without them. Heaven's Hero conquered death!

I know this is true, because death has gotten personal with me. Many of you dear readers were aware of this, and have prayed for and encouraged me through these years with notes and letters sharing your own experiences. How I have treasured such understanding. For the death of one dearly loved thrusts a rapier thorn. First I lost my dear mom, and later my dad to cancer. Then I had to watch my precious husband die. I will probably never experience a moment in life when I feel deeper pain or keener joy than I did in that terrible, wonderful moment. I saw him leave his body along with his last gasping breath, felt the cold, frightening finality of death . . . like someone slamming the door on laughter and love. Sobs burst from within me at the horror of sin's ultimate stabbing.

Then joy erupted from the well of my soul, bathing my sorrow in waves of gratitude. As I wept, I sobbed, "Thank You! Thank You! Oh, thank You, dear Jesus, for Your cross! Thank You for the empty tomb!" This implausible, outrageous joy let me see and know in the deepest most hurting part of my soul that Herb had passed from this life to life everlasting. This was not the end! Everything in me was awash in the pain and wonder of that truth.

From Christ's death and resurrection blossomed life everlasting for everyone who will believe and receive His incredible gift. "For God so loved the world that He gave His one and only Son, that whoever believes in Him shall not perish, but have eternal life" (John 3:16). What joy!

So together, we who have believed and received can marvel at the flowers that blossom amid sin's manure in this world. In His heavenly economy, God uses everything for our ultimate good and His ultimate glory. He knows how to deal with thorns. He knows how to force them to bloom into salvation and life.

We can trust Him as we learn to sip the sweet nectar of joy that God squeezes for us from the fruit of life's thorn bushes. For we know that this world's piercing pain will soon be gone forever. Together, we can learn to "lick honey off a thorn"! We can learn to really live while we live!

Because Jesus said, "A thief is only there to steal and kill and destroy. I came so they can have real and eternal life, more and better life than they ever dreamed of" (John 10:10 *The Message*).

Optimist, Pessimist, or Realist?

THE REALITY, HOWEVER, IS FOUND IN CHRIST.
PAUL, COLOSSIANS 2:17

STRANGELY, it was while sitting in my dentist's waiting room thumbing through an old magazine that I discovered the real theme of this book. Although the book was half written by then, I still didn't fully understand what I was trying to say about living life well in this world of pain and joy.

But a magazine article containing a thought-provoking quote captured my attention, brought a smile to my face, and led me to sudden understanding. So this was what I was ultimately writing about!

When I was summoned into the doctor's office, I waved the magazine before him and thanked him for helping me to define the purpose statement of my book. I showed him the quote that had intrigued me by Julie K. Norem, a psychology professor at Wellesley College. "Pessimists are more likely to be right," she said. "Optimists are more likely to be happy."

"So which are you then, an optimist, or a pessimist?" he asked with a laugh.

"Both, I think. Actually, I'm trying hard to be a realist," I said. "They didn't cover that category in this article. But I just realized that's what my latest book is all about . . . seeking to be an open-eyed, hope-filled, realist in a world of both pain and joy."

He thought he might be interested in such a book. And if

I had been further along in the process I could have told him a little more of what the book is and isn't about. I could have said:

This book is all about living as a realist in a world that stabs and hurts us, and yet is dripping with the honey of God's hope, presence, and power to change and bless us in the midst.

This book is not about pretending life is any better or worse than it is. It's not just about the benefits of focusing on the good things in order to reduce the power the bad things have over us. It's not only about milking the tough stuff for all its wisdom and worth.

This book is about the importance of looking at all of life and living it all the way through to eternity. It is a call to those of us who would close our eyes and run away from the pain; as well as for those who want to camp in pleasures and good memories, denying the brokenness. And it is a challenge to those of us with a tendency to focus on life's losses, losing joy and victory in the process. In short, this book is for me. This book is my gradual, random realization on paper that it is only those with a true knowledge of God who are able to be functioning, healthy realists. And even with God, life can be very, very difficult. Any honest realist without the hope of God is bound to end up in despair or denial.

It occurs to me that, similar to the way in which this book presented itself, life comes to us in daily pages that don't always offer an organized or obvious theme. We live through different issues, events, and phases that may not seem to make a complete story with a sensible beginning, middle, and end. But we take the laughter and tears however they come, and let our God of Reality make sense of it all. And He will. That's His promise to us. Believing this truth, and living in this truth, is the daily challenge of being a realist who has met God.

We need to unflinchingly receive it all—all the good and

bad of life—and repeatedly choose to know that God really loves us and is constantly at work for our good and His glory. And while it isn't easy to live in the conviction of this truth, we haven't much else of real worth to give to our Maker, have we? It is our privilege to give at least this much back to Him.

God calls this kind of living reality "faith," And it is His gold standard. It is all He asks of us until we leave this earth and no longer need to give Him anything except unending face-to-face praise. For now we give Him upturned faith-to-face praise.

What a God we have! And how fortunate we are to have him, this Father of our Master Jesus! Because Jesus was raised from the dead, we've been given a brand-new life and have everything to live for, including a future in heaven—and the future starts now! God is keeping careful watch over us and the future. The Day is coming when you'll have it all—life healed and whole.

I know how great this makes you feel, even though you have to put up with every kind of aggravation in the meantime. Pure gold put in the fire comes out of it proved pure; genuine faith put through this suffering comes out proved genuine. When Jesus wraps this all up, it's your faith, not your gold, that God will have on display as evidence of his victory.

You never saw him, yet you love him. You still don't see him, yet you trust him—with laughter and singing. Because you kept on believing, you'll get what you're looking forward to: total salvation.

1 Peter 1:3—9 The Message

A Family of Shining Realists

I WANT TO MAKE GOD SMILE, AND I WANT
TO LIVE BEFORE OTHERS SO THAT WHEN THEY
SEE ME, THEY WILL SMILE AT GOD.

DR. AMBA MPUTELA

SOME of us are born directly onto a bed of thorns. At least that's what it feels like. Our world hurts—seems always to have hurt. We are wounded and wary. Sometimes, justifying our rage at the neglect and abuse, we pass the hurt around. Life isn't fair in a fallen world.

Others, initially more fortunate, slide softly onto a bed of roses, then discover with dismay that life's cozy cradle holds harsh thorns of reality. Things wilt and die. Sharp words and acts by unkind or unthinking people cut into self-worth and confidence. Loss slices through our world. We can become self-protective and guarded—filled with resentment that life turned and stung us. Life isn't fair in this sin-riddled world.

It is into such realities as these that our Savior was born. Jesus landed on a bed of scratchy stable straw, reaching out His hands for our spikes of sin, bowing His head to receive our crown of thorns. In Him the reality of righteousness met and conquered the reality of sin. But it was a painful battle. Jesus knew that sin was no small thorn. By our own choice, it had pierced us through the heart. And now, by His choice, it would pierce Him. Truly this wasn't fair. But God's amazing grace superseded "fairness." Mercy triumphed over justice.

Why did Jesus choose to make His bed on this earth? What prompted Him to accept such a painful assignment on our behalf? Why did He allow sin to stab Him to death, willingly taking our place?

In unfathomable love, Christ took our thorns of death to make of us a brand-new, eternal family of honest people, re-created in the image of God. He asks us to live transparently in the sweetness of His Spirit while still in this world of sin and brokenness. We are redeemed by our risen and living Savior, to shine like stars in the world's darkness. We are to offer the sweet fragrance of the hope of Christ to nostrils filled with the stench of death. We are to be like drops of honey, tempting a world to taste of God's eternal life and goodness.

Christ died to make us a family of shining realists...

- people who know where we're headed, but recognize we're not there yet.
- people who don't pretend that victory means lack of pain and struggle.
- people who laugh, and love, and give anyway.
- people who refuse to live in denial or fear.
- people willing to walk through the muck with Jesus.
- people who see clearly that the fruits of heaven and hell coexist on this earth.
- people who know that such a world offers great opportunity for God's grace.
- people who make God smile and live in a way that makes others smile at God.
- people who know how to lick honey off a thorn.

"In this world you will have trouble. But take heart! I have over-come the world."   Jesus, John 16:33

For this reason I kneel before the Father, from whom his whole family in heaven and on earth derives its name. I pray that out of his glorious riches he may strengthen you with power through his Spirit in your inner being, so that Christ may dwell in your hearts through faith. . . .

Be imitators of God, therefore, as dearly loved children, and live a life of love, just as Christ loved us and gave himself up for us as a fragrant offering and sacrifice to God. . . . Live as children of light.   Ephesians 3:14–17; 5:1–2, 8

Balanced Between
Heaven and Earth

I DESIRE TO HAVE BOTH HEAVEN AND HELL
EVER IN MY EYE, WHILE I STAND ON THIS
ISTHMUS OF LIFE, BETWEEN TWO BOUNDLESS
OCEANS.   —JOHN WESLEY

Lord Jesus,
in this world You walked
a balanced way,
sinless among sinners—
giving Yourself away
without coming apart—
living before the Father in
humble confidence—
shouting Your holiness in
whispers of love—
pushing through the agony to
the joy set before You.
Oh, how I need Your grace to
walk as You did,
ever poised and balanced with
one foot on earth,
the other in heaven.

"I'm not asking you to take them out of the world, but to keep them safe from Satan's power. They are not part of this world any more than I am. Make them pure and holy through teaching them your words of truth. As you sent me into the world, I am sending them into the world, and I consecrate myself to meet their need for growth in truth and holiness.

"I am not praying for these alone but also for the future believers who will come to me because of the testimony of these. My prayer for all of them is that they will be of one heart and mind, just as you and I are, Father—that just as you are in me and I am in you, so they will be in us, and the world will believe you sent me.

"I have given them the glory you gave me—the glorious unity of being one, as we are—I in them and you in me, all being perfected into one—so that the world will know you sent me and will understand that you love them as much as you love me."

Jesus, praying for us, John 17:15–23 TLB

Power Supply Shortage

JESUS ANSWERED, "WITHOUT ME YOU CAN
DO NOTHING" (JOHN 15:5). YET WE ACT, FOR
THE MOST PART, AS THOUGH WITHOUT US
GOD CAN DO NOTHING.

LORETTA ROSS-GOTTA

I WAS having an energy crisis. I had spent a considerable amount of my emotional and spiritual energy that morning indulging in uncharitable thoughts toward our local energy supplier because, frankly, they weren't "supplying."

The power in my home had gone out for the fourth day in less than a week. This meant: stop writing and pray that I hadn't lost anything on my computer, reset all my clocks again, re-program the sprinkler system, and . . . well, you know the drill.

So I picked up the only phone that functions without electricity and called our amazing San Diego Gas & (sometimes even) Electric Company to find out why they raise their rates through the roof, then drop their service through the floor.

After waiting on hold, and failing to use the time to pray about my attitude, I finally heard a measured, electronic voice suggest a whole menu of buttons I might enjoy pressing.

"To open a new account, press 1."

"To inquire about your bill, press 2."

And so on, until, finally—

"To report an interruption in service, press 7."

Or was it 27? Whatever. At least I might finally get to talk to somebody. So I press a number.

"If you live in the Northern Hemisphere of the world, press 1 . . ."

I never did find my way through the maze to a human being, so I finally hung up and plopped my bad attitude down on the living room couch for a good sulk. Then, even though I hadn't pressed a single button, I got a message.

"You don't like this, Susan. But the truth is, you've sometimes wished that I offered menu options, haven't you? Like when you're sitting at your computer trying to write and failing miserably. Or when you're frustrated because you haven't even gotten as far as sitting at the keyboard. When you finally remember to call on Me to report trouble, you don't really want to talk with Me. You'd rather hear,

"For inspiration dropped directly onto paper, press 1."

"For the perfect verb, press 2."

"For scheduling problems, press 3."

"For a decent power supply, press 4."

He sure had my number!

God's system isn't "automated"—never has been and never will be. When we finally remember to call Him about our power outage, He says, "Stay on the line—I'll continue to be right with you."

To get the help we need, we have to stay connected to the unfailing Power Supply, the True Vine, the Author of Life. All writing, living, loving, and giving must be the overflow of that relationship.

There are no other "menu options."

"Remain in me, and I will remain in you. No branch can bear fruit by itself; it must remain in the vine. Neither can you bear fruit unless you remain in me.

"I am the vine; you are the branches. If a man remains in me and I in him, he will bear much fruit; apart from me you can do nothing. . . . If you remain in me and my words remain in you, ask whatever you wish, and it will be given you. This is to my Father's glory, that you bear much fruit, showing yourselves to be my disciples.

"As the Father has loved me, so have I loved you. Now remain in my love." John 15:4–5, 7–9

Call to me and I will answer you and tell you great and unsearchable things you do not know. Jeremiah 33:3

How Sweet It Is!

A GOOD LAUGH IS SUNSHINE IN THE HOUSE.
WILLIAM THACKERAY

ONE night while I was cooking dinner and Herb was talking to me from the family room couch, I suddenly became aware that he had stopped talking. I looked up and saw tears coursing down his face.

Switching off the stove, I went and sat beside him, encircling him in my arms as I waited for the flood to subside. I thought I knew what I'd hear when he was able to speak. At that time, his cancer was going into what turned out to be a brief remission due to the double hormonal therapy the doctors were administering. We were both coping with the effects of this treatment, as well as the normal fear attendant to life-threatening cancer. I expected he needed to talk about some of these things.

"What is it, Honey?" I gently encouraged.

Finally my strapping German engineer husband wiped his eyes, blew his nose hard, and wailed, "I don't know! I'm not crying about the cancer or anything. That's the worst part of this!" Then as though each word deserved special emphasis, he nearly yelled, "I don't even know why I'm crying! I'm just . . . crying!"

He wiped away more tears, then finally asked, meekly, "Do you think it's the hormones?"

Fighting my own little battle to maintain composure—I was afraid of laughing, not crying—I said, "It probably is the hormones. Since your medication is suppressing all testosterone production so that the cancer can't feed on it, you're probably left with only a few female hormones. And unfortunately, female hormones are more prone to have tears in them."

"You know," he said thoughtfully but with resolve, "men are too hard on women! They really don't understand! You can't help it . . . you just have to cry sometimes! Men should to be nicer to women."

I lost the fight and burst out laughing. "Oh, honey," I gasped, "If I could just wrap you up and take you to women's retreats when I'm speaking! I could auction you off for big bucks!"

Surely, I could have come up with something a bit more compassionate to say. But this was some of the sweetest honey any miserable thorn could offer a woman. This, and the fact that we were now both experiencing hot flashes! And so we laughed. In the midst of it all, we laughed, and cried, and hugged, and went forward.

Life is a gift from God. Enjoying life is a gift we can give back to Him. It is good to laugh, and love, and live, as long as there is life.

> *Live happily with the woman you love through the fleeting days of life, for the wife God gives you is your best reward down here for all your earthly toil.*   *Ecclesiastes 9:9 TLB*

> *A cheerful heart is good medicine, but a crushed spirit dries up the bones.*   *Proverbs 17:22*

> *Even in laughter the heart may ache, and joy may end in grief.*   *Proverbs 14:13*

> *There is a time for everything, and a season for every activity under heaven: . . . a time to weep and a time to laugh, a time to mourn and a time to dance.*   *Ecclesiastes 3:1, 4*

Where You Find Me

IF YOUR HEART IS BROKEN, YOU'LL FIND
YAHWEH RIGHT THERE; IF YOU'RE KICKED
IN THE GUT, HE'LL HELP YOU CATCH YOUR
BREATH.   PSALM 34:18 THE MESSAGE

Did you know, My child, that
where you find Me
determines what you know of Me?
I am vast, yet intimate and present.
When you find Me in your busy days,
you discover the Lord of daily things.
In chaos and crisis,
I come as peace and control.
In creation's abundance,
delight in My beauty and order.
In sin and failure,
revel in My grace and power to save.
In loss and heartache,
rest in My compassion and love.
When you go to the depths,
you find Me deeper still.
There is always more of Me.
I wait to be discovered.

*Can you fathom the mysteries of God? Can you probe the limits
of the Almighty?*   Job 11:7

*We know about these things because God has sent his Spirit to
tell us, and his Spirit searches out and shows us all of God's
deepest secrets. No one can really know what anyone else is
thinking, or what he is really like, except that person himself.
And no one can know God's thoughts except God's own Spirit.
And God has actually given us his Spirit (not the world's spirit)
to tell us about the wonderful free gifts of grace and blessing that
God has given us.*
                                      1 Corinthians 2:10–12, TLB

The Twig Heart Message

HE SENDS FROM HEAVEN AND SAVES ME . . .
GOD SENDS HIS LOVE AND HIS FAITHFULNESS.

PSALM 57:3

I HAD come to dread Sundays. Worshiping without Herb beside me was a constantly painful reminder that after thirty-two years of marriage, I was a widow. And leaving church alone got harder as the weeks went by, with the afternoon stretching bleak and empty before me. Sunday had always been our special day together.

We had established the marriage strengthening tradition of spending this day together enjoying and discovering God, one another, and our beautiful city of San Diego. Then cancer came, and when it finally left, it took him away from me—on a Sunday evening. Now, of all the days in the week, this was the saddest. It was the day I doggedly counted my blessings just to make it through.

I would count the rare blessing of having all three of my wonderful grown children living nearby. Herb always felt this showed their basic good sense, reasoning, "Why would they choose to move anywhere else when they already live in paradise?"

Sunday became the day I recited the truth that God promised to be with me always. I frequently thanked Him for placing me in a church family of beloved brothers and sisters in Christ. I would remind myself that although I was lonely, I was not really alone.

Other times I would find comfort in the truth that Herb and I—though he was not physically beside me—were still one in Christ, still worshiping and praising God together—though from separate places.

But one Sunday the truth and pain of sorrow simply outweighed my ability to counterbalance it with the truth of God's blessings. Dejectedly, I shuffled up the sidewalk toward my car thinking, *Lord, I know there's much to be thankful for, and I know that You love and care for me, but it's just not the same thing. I miss Herb! I miss being special to him. I miss his love. And oh, how I miss our Sundays together.* Then the toe of my shoe bumped into something.

A twig lay at my feet, blown from one of the eucalyptus trees near our church. It had been split down the middle and, as it dried, it had curled into the shape of a heart. I had never seen anything like it. I bent to pick it up. A single, slender leaf clung to one edge thrusting itself through the center of the heart. It was a broken heart.

I knew then that I held in my hand a love note from God and Herb. It was okay to have a broken heart. I felt understood. I also felt fresh hope. Healing would come.

The Lord's "twig heart message" hangs on my kitchen wall now, a constant reminder of the communion of compassion from the God of all comfort. The One who sent His Son to die on a tree had used the twig of a tree to tell me He understands the ache of separation. With His heart of love, He reminded my lonely heart that weeping endures for a season, but love endures forever.

Record my lament; list my tears on your scroll—are they not in your record? Psalm 56:8

"I, even I, am he who comforts you." Isaiah 51:12

Praise be to the God and Father of our Lord Jesus Christ, the Father of compassion and the God of all comfort, who comforts us in all our troubles, so that we can comfort those in any trouble with the comfort we ourselves have received from God. For just as the sufferings of Christ flow over into our lives, so also through Christ our comfort overflows.   2 Corinthians 1:3–5

For I am convinced that neither death nor life, neither angels nor demons, neither the present nor the future, nor any powers, neither height nor depth, nor anything else in all creation, will be able to separate us from the love of God that is in Christ Jesus our Lord.

Romans 8:38–39

The Shepherd Search

YOUR ROD AND YOUR STAFF, THEY COMFORT
ME.   DAVID, PSALM 23:4

How is it that our
troubles and pain so naturally
curve into clamoring question-marks
barbed and aimed at God?
  "Where are You?"
    "What are You doing?"
      "Why are You hiding from me?"
        "Don't You love me anymore?"
And our frantic demands
muffle the Shepherd's searching voice.
  "Precious one, where are you?"
    "What are you doing?"
      "Why are you hiding from Me?"
        "Don't you love Me anymore?"
For the curve of our Shepherd's questions
is the crook of His staff reaching to
draw us to His side.

For the Lord God says: "I will search and find my sheep. I will
be like a shepherd looking for his flock. I will find my sheep and
rescue them from all the places they were scattered in that dark

and cloudy day. And I will bring them back. . . . Yes, I will
give them good pasture on the high hills of Israel. There they
will lie down in peace and feed in luscious mountain pastures.
I myself will be the Shepherd of my sheep and cause them to lie
down in peace," the Lord God says. "I will seek my lost ones,
those who strayed away, and bring them safely home again. I
will put splints and bandages upon their broken limbs and heal
the sick." Ezekiel 34:11—16 TLB

He will stand and shepherd his flock in the strength of the LORD,
in the majesty of the name of the LORD *his God. And they will*
live securely, for then his greatness will reach to the ends of the
earth. And he will be their peace. Micah 5:4—5

Dear Grieving One

LOSS AND SUFFERING, JOYFULLY ACCEPTED
FOR THE KINGDOM OF GOD, SHOW THE
SUPREMACY OF GOD'S WORTH MORE CLEARLY
IN THE WORLD THAN ALL THE WORSHIP AND
PRAYER.   JOHN PIPER

AS I pray for you, I see God there with you—the Answer Who doesn't always speak the answers, but just is. He is holding you tenderly in His arms and pressing you close to His great heartbeat of compassion, letting His tears mingle with yours. His sweet breath is gently ruffling your hair with wordless whispers of hope in the night.

Let Him hold you for as long as it takes. Thank Him for all the wonderful people He has brought into your life over the years, and let them hold you for as long as it takes. You might need to explain that you need them to listen and care, but not try to fix you or make the pain go away. They will be helped as they share your hurt, and so will you.

Cry as much and as often as you need or want to. Weeping is not weakness. Feeling as though you're "falling apart" is not an indication of a failing testimony. Doubts and questions don't insult or frighten God, so speak freely to Him. He wants your whole heart, even if it comes to Him in broken, jagged pieces.

There are no "timetables" on grief. There is no "right way" for everyone to grieve. But there are some things you can do to move through grief in healthy ways. Like taking care of yourself, asking for prayer, facing rather than avoiding the pain, perhaps joining a grief support group, constantly leaning on God, and thanking and praising Him as you inch forward. But they're not quick fixes.

There may be those who suggest that deep or prolonged grief—with its attendant doubts, questions, and often anger—indicates a lack of trust in God or a failure to rely on Him. They believe that stoic bravery or a "quick recovery" is a credit to God's reputation and yours. Perhaps they think that refusing to express painful feelings is a way to snuff them out. They don't understand. We are glad they haven't yet had reason to.

Lack of trust will, indeed, prolong the pain and isolate us from God's full comfort, but feelings of doubt, rage, or engulfing loneliness come even to those who fully trust God. It is a part of honest grief to express them before the Lord.

Knowing that your loved one is with God doesn't erase the agony that he or she is no longer with you on this earth. Knowing that Christ conquered death eternally doesn't nullify the pain of separation now. God created the process of grief as His path through the losses of this sin-riddled world. The integrity of emotional and spiritual honesty requires us to walk that painful but hope-filled path.

Try writing letters to God and letters to your loved one. Often that helps. And expect to deal with a sense of confusion at times, even some inertia, for this is common. I can't tell you how many times I would go into a room and have no idea why I had gone there. I tend to do that on occasion anyway, but I did it again and again in the first weeks after Herb died. Deep grief is disorienting.

Be gentle with yourself. Don't rush into big changes. Eat right. Buy tons of soft Kleenex. Ask people for patience when you forget everything from their name to what you told them you would do. Wait in—not just on, but in—the Lord, and rest there. You don't have to do everything the way you used to do it. Concentrate on putting one foot in front of the other, living one moment at a time. After all, that's all we can ever live anyway.

Take to heart Jesus' words that "each day has enough trouble of its own," and consciously work at not taking on the whole load of frightening tomorrows. For Jesus is already living in tomorrow, working things out on your behalf. He is working at a leisurely pace. He's not nervous or concerned. He is preparing a table for you—with candlelight and roses and wonderful food—in the presence of your enemies. What a God, who sets up His dining room on the battlefront!

But even knowing these things, there will be times when you may fear that you won't survive the pain and waves of grief. But you will. Because God will not let go of you. He is faithful in this, too. Especially in this.

I celebrate with you those moments when you'll know and feel His precious presence, and I hold on in faith for you in those moments when you won't know or feel a thing but pain. Just remember, He is the same yesterday, today, and forever. And He loves you with a love that will not—indeed, cannot—let you go. There is healing in His wings. I know, for He has lifted me up on those healing wings.

Be merciful to me, O LORD, for I am in distress; my eyes grow weak with sorrow, my soul and my body with grief. Psalm 31:9

Though he brings grief, he will show compassion, so great is his unfailing love. For he does not willingly bring affliction or grief to the children of men. Lamentations 3:32–33

He will cover you with his feathers, and under his wings you will find refuge; his faithfulness will be your shield and rampart. Psalm 91:4

Where Is Your Heart Today?

NOW IS YOUR TIME OF GRIEF, BUT I WILL SEE
YOU AGAIN AND YOU WILL REJOICE, AND NO
ONE WILL TAKE AWAY YOUR JOY.

JESUS, JOHN 16:22

Where is your heart today, My child?
Has it left you to follow,
   weeping, after that precious
     part of you that I have
      taken home?
Your aching heart seeks that place
  where your dear one
   dances and sings beneath the
    shadow of My wing.
One day, when your weeping slows,
  and your heart wanders back to you
feeling bereft and stunned to silence by its
    singularity,
  it will make the wonderful discovery—
one that your head has long known—
   that you, too, can live on
(though you haven't wanted to, I know).
And right there, alone in your house, you will learn to
  dance and sing again
   beneath the shadow of My wing.
Then your heart, too, will be home, My love.

On my bed I remember you; I think of you through the watches of the night. Because you are my help, I sing in the shadow of your wings. My soul clings to you; your right hand upholds me.

Psalm 63:6–8

Saying this often helped me. Substitute the name of your loved one who is with the Lord:

(Herb) is no longer on earth, therefore I hurt and grieve,
yet I rejoice that (Herb) is with You, Lord.
I am still on earth and though I hurt and grieve,
yet I rejoice that You, Lord, are with me.
So, in a deep, untouchable way, (Herb) and I are together still.
Forever together in Christ.

Good Things from the Heart

GOOD PEOPLE BRING GOOD THINGS OUT OF
THE GOOD THEY STORED IN THEIR HEARTS.
                    JESUS, LUKE 6:45 NCV

PEOPLE amazed me in the good things they found to do to
encourage and help us when Herb was so sick. Other than their
medical services, the hospice personnel never had to send any
other volunteers to our home. There was nothing for them to
do. The place was crawling with God's people honoring Him by
putting His love into action.

In shifts, friends brought delicious meals, cleaned my house,
answered the door and phone, and did the washing so that I
could stay by Herb's bedside. Almost before soiled sheets hit the
floor, they were back, clean and neatly folded. People came and
sang, prayed, talked, listened, laughed, cried, and loved us.

Toward the end, when someone needed to be with Herb
constantly, a couple of friends who are nurses took the night
shifts so that I could get some sleep. One had to go to work the
next day, but did it anyway. Another flew in from hundreds of
miles away to take the night shift for a week. Another couple
offered to pay for a night nurse if needed.

Encouraging cards filled an entire wall beside Herb's bed. One
day a new nurse's aide came to tend Herb and said, "Oh, I've heard
about this wall of cards! The word's getting around about this place
and all your wonderful Christian friends." I think God smiled.

A cheerful nurse breezed into the bedroom one morning with this question: "Am I seeing things, or is that actually the wife of our Chief of Neurology dusting your living room?" She had seen correctly—the doctor and his wife are friends from church, and she wanted to help.

One day Herb wished out loud that he could have a haircut, so a friend from church said, "I cut my husband's hair. If you don't think he looks too bad, I'll be happy to cut yours, too." Herb thought he looked pretty good. So she went home and came back with scissors and a cape, and Herb got his haircut, right there in bed.

Another day, very near the end, Herb wished he could sit one last time with me at the edge of our backyard canyon view. So my sons carried him in his wheelchair down the stairs and took him outside where he made one last toast to life.

The loving creativity that people poured into their acts touched me the most deeply. One day my daughter-in-law brought a basin filled with soapy water and gave me a pedicure as I sat at Herb's bedside. I thought of Jesus washing the disciples' feet.

Another time the Praise Team from our church came with guitars and filled our bedroom with joyful singing that gave Herb a little prelude of where he was headed, and took us along. At Christmastime, the youth came caroling.

Our creative and loving pastor's wife tended the flowers being delivered. The flowers that remained fresh, she tucked into a live ivy wreath she had made to greet visitors with a touch of beauty at our front door. One day her youngest teenage daughter asked what Herb's "view" was—what he "looked at" all day? Her Mom told her that his hospital bed was facing our upstairs bedroom window, so he probably saw treetops, rooftops, and the sky. Then this delightful girl said, "He probably gets tired of looking at the same thing all the time." So she asked her mom to get some colorful helium balloons, put them on very long ribbons, and tie them to the bushes below so they would float and dance in front of his window for a change of scene. He loved it. (This same girl gave me a cuddly teddy bear to hug after Herb died, calling it the "Finefrock Bear" after my maiden name.)

Another day the doorbell rang. A dear woman from church stood there looking a bit awkward, holding a small red and white basket. "I don't know what you'll think of this," she said, "but since tomorrow's Valentine's Day, and since I couldn't imagine you out doing any shopping . . . well, I sort of picked out little gifts—nothing much, really. And there are cards for you to give to each other. I had a hard time knowing what cards you might choose, but I did the best I could."

It was difficult not to cry with gratitude as she handed me the colorful little beribboned basket with its three small wrapped packages and two brown lunch sacks containing the cards. The bags said, "For Sue to give to Herb" and "For Herb to give to Sue." One gift was tagged for him, one for me, and the other was for both of us. How wonderful! I couldn't wait to find out what I gave Herb.

I hugged her hard and took the basket upstairs. I gave Herb the bag that held his card for me, along with a pen. Then I took my own and went to another room and, through tears, tried to write in it what there were no words to say.

The next day we exchanged our cards and gifts. Although the cancer had metastasized, affecting Herb's eyesight and even some of his brain function, he had managed to painstakingly scrawl his Valentine message on the bottom of my card. He had crossed out and rewritten words in an effort to express his deep love for me and his gratitude that one day we would be together again in the presence of God. It was essentially the same message I had written to him. I held in my hand a treasure beyond belief, because within three weeks he was gone from me. The creative love of one woman had given me this last, and lasting, love gift.

What was in the wrapped gifts we gave to one another? It turns out that I gave him "Male Toner Tea," and he gave me "Female Toner Tea." The other gift was a music tape of "Yanni Live at the Acropolis." So I made us each a cup of our respective teas, turned on the music, and we had a little Valentine Tea. I'd say it was our last Valentine Tea, but it was also our first.

Ah, creative love that gives such delightful moments and memories! It's the fruit that reveals who and what we are, and then goes to heaven before us.

"No good tree bears bad fruit, nor does a bad tree bear good fruit. Each tree is recognized by its own fruit. People do not pick figs from thornbushes, or grapes from briers."

Jesus, Luke 6:43—44

Now he who supplies seed to the sower and bread for food will also supply and increase your store of seed and will enlarge the harvest of your righteousness. You will be made rich in every way so that you can be generous on every occasion, and through us your generosity will result in thanksgiving to God.

This service that you perform is not only supplying the needs of God's people but is also overflowing in many expressions of thanks to God. Because of the service by which you have proved yourselves, men will praise God for the obedience that accompanies your confession of the gospel of Christ, and for your generosity in sharing with them and with everyone else. And in their prayers for you their hearts will go out to you, because of the surpassing grace God has given you. Thanks be to God for his indescribable gift!

2 Corinthians 9:10—15

Painfully Sweet Partings

HOW NATURAL IT IS THAT I SHOULD FEEL AS
I DO ABOUT YOU, FOR YOU HAVE A VERY SPE-
CIAL PLACE IN MY HEART. WE HAVE SHARED
TOGETHER THE BLESSINGS OF GOD.
                    PAUL, PHILIPPIANS 1:7 TLB

WHEN someone dear leaves us—whether he moves to some distant spot on this earth, or beyond this earth into God's presence—we feel our hearts being pulled apart.

Everything within us cries out, "But I have you in my heart, and you are taking part of my heart away with you!"

Yet this loved one won't leave my heart just because he leaves my presence. Still, I will have to live without his daily touch. And that hurts. It requires adjustments I don't want to make. I don't want to have to learn to live without this friend, this loved one! But that is what grieving must accomplish.

Grief is the work of adjusting to loss—learning to live with precious memories, when I'd far rather be living with the precious person. Yet, as I inch and finally stride forward, I find that I am left with something more than just memories. His love continues to reach out and touch me daily.

Sometimes we don't fully realize how much of themselves people have deposited in us until distance or death forces us apart, and we begin to look within at what is left behind. It is then that we weep and, at the same time, thank and praise God in the midst of the pain. Because we realize that the love invested in us is with us to stay.

We begin to understand that, in Christ, we are ever present. It may be one of the most precious gifts inherited by the children of the ever present "I Am." And this gift is ours whether the enemy is death, the inevitable changes and losses of time, or a moving van.

When a loved one dies, I carry the part of that person that lives in my heart on into God's presence on earth, continuing to touch the lives of many. While the person who has died carries the part of me that lives in their heart directly into God's glorious presence. We are still together.

The same truth applies when our pain is caused because a loved one must move to some distant place on this earth. Whatever that person has invested in me stays behind and continues to live and love here. And what I have invested in that person travels within him or her to touch the lives of others.

Parting is truly such sweet sorrow. We separate, but we are never really apart. Eternity has begun in our hearts!

*Only God knows how deep is my love and longing for you—
with the tenderness of Jesus Christ.*   *Philippians 1:8 TLB*

*May God bless you all. Yes, I pray that God our Father and
the Lord Jesus Christ will give each of you his fullest blessings
and his peace in your hearts and your lives. Philippians 1:2 TLB*

A Tsunami of His Peace

MAY THE LORD OF PEACE HIMSELF GIVE YOU
PEACE AT ALL TIMES AND IN EVERY WAY.
2 THESSALONIANS 3:16

AN encouraging note came to me signed, "In a tsunami of His shalom." I loved it! Shalom is God's sweet greeting of peace, and my pastor friend, Dennis Baker, had just sent me an absolute tidal wave of it!

Yet, the more I thought about it, the more unlikely the phrase seemed. How do "tsunami" and "peace" fit in the same sentence?

The tsunami is no ordinary big wave. It is "a very large ocean wave generated by an underwater earthquake or volcanic eruption." It's a huge wall of rushing water produced by something shaking and altering the depths. This is peace? Change happening in the depths where no one sees, but is so profound that it washes surface things away?

It sounds like the Almighty at work. And for many of us, that is both our biggest fear and our greatest hope. We long for, and dread, such deep, soul-shaking work by the Spirit of God who hovers over the deep waters to bring about His eternal change that produces true eternal harmony and contentment.

What if I'm washed away in the tidal wave? What if I lose myself? What if I die?

Jesus said that I would. Then He explained that the one who loses his life, finds it. He said that the one who dies to self, truly lives. We don't want to understand that Jesus won our peace on the battlefield of death and resurrection, and that we will win it the same way. We want to think the peace of Christ will slip comfortably into the cracks of our cluttered, distracted lives. But that would require a piece of Christ, and He doesn't come in pieces. Real peace requires room to reign.

When we allow our Creator to wash across the landscape of our lives with His powerful surge, it becomes a wave of true shalom. God's tsunami salvation sweeps away those things that distract, deaden, divide, defeat, and kill. It is a cleansing flood that carries away the fears and frustrations that imprison and destroy. It leaves us clean and new, with plenty of space for God to build His eternal stuff.

Why do we most fear the very shakeup needed to generate true and lasting order and rest? We tell ourselves that we are "keeping the peace" but the truth is, there is very little peace to keep. Sometimes we spend our whole lives trying to avoid the big eruption needed to release God's peace like a flood. We settle for those small swells that come regularly on Sunday mornings.

Dare we ask, "What am I struggling to avoid? What disappointment lies buried beneath this ocean of tears, shed or unshed? What deep unrest stirs the surface of my soul making waves—always making waves—but not waves of peace?"

Dare we trust the One who is our Peace to catch us up in His tsunami? We will be swept into His arms and finally led beside the still waters we have longed for. A tsunami of His shalom, dear one!

If you had obeyed me, you would have had peace like a full-flowing river. Good things would have flowed to you like the waves of the sea.   Isaiah 48:18 NCV

Wash away all my iniquity and cleanse me from my sin.
                                                                              Psalm 51:2

For he will come like a pent-up flood that the breath of the LORD drives along.
     "The Redeemer will come to those...who repent of their sins," declares the LORD.   Isaiah 59:19–20

Deep calls to deep in the roar of your waterfalls; all your waves and breakers have swept over me.   Psalm 42:7

"Peace I leave with you; my peace I give you. I do not give to you as the world gives. Do not let your hearts be troubled and do not be afraid."   John 14:27

"Test me in this," says the LORD Almighty, "and see if I will not throw open the floodgates of heaven and pour out so much bless-ing that you will not have room enough for it."   Malachi 3:10

The IN Crwd

FOR IN CHRIST ALL THE FULLNESS OF THE
DEITY LIVES IN BODILY FORM, AND YOU HAVE
BEEN GIVEN FULLNESS IN CHRIST, WHO IS THE
HEAD OVER EVERY POWER AND AUTHORITY.
PAUL, COLOSSIANS 2:9–10

INcluded
INside His arms
INscribed with His Name
INseparable
INcomprehensible love
INcredible peace
INdescribable joy
INdestructible riches
IN touch with Truth
INcreased in faith
INfused with hope
INcarnate strength
INstructed to serve
INspired to live
IN endless praise
IN Christ

Therefore, if anyone is in Christ, he is a new creation; the old has gone, the new has come!   2 Corinthians 5:17

I always thank God for you because of his grace given you in Christ Jesus. For in him you have been enriched in every way— in all your speaking and in all your knowledge.
1 Corinthians 1:4–5

No matter how many promises God has made, they are "Yes" in Christ. And so through him the "Amen" is spoken by us to the glory of God. Now it is God who makes both us and you stand firm in Christ. He anointed us, set his seal of ownership on us, and put his Spirit in our hearts as a deposit, guaranteeing what is to come.   2 Corinthians 1:20–22

My love to all of you in Christ Jesus.   1 Corinthians 16:24

The Fog of Forgetfulness

I PROBABLY HAD THE PERFECT QUOTE TO GO
WITH THIS, BUT I CAN'T REMEMBER FOR SURE.
SL

RECENTLY I was involved in a conversation with a friend when she was seized with a single violent sneeze. After exclaiming over the suddenness and force of it, she said, "Okay now, where were we? I think that sneeze just blew everything right out of my head! It's terrible how I lose my train of thought lately—I'm in a fog half the time. You know, I see a lot of people, older than us, who don't seem to have any problem completing a thought. Have you noticed that? Do you think that means our minds clear up as we get older? I sure hope so. Now, what was it we were talking about before?"

But I didn't know. Because I'd stopped to say, "Bless you!" and had lost my train of thought too.

So we decided that friends in the "Fifties Fog" should travel together in packs of at least three at all times. That way, if somebody sneezes, and somebody blesses her, there's somebody left to explain what was going on before it happened. It may be the only way, we decided, that we'll be able to carry on lucid conversations that reach any kind of satisfactory conclusion.

It was an idea with real value. I knew this from another recent experience. I had been standing with two other women after a meeting while one was explaining to the other, who had just admired her lapel pin, that it was a gift from her mother—an early Christmas present.

Fortunately, I was there to remind her that it was not her mother, but I who had given it to her during a particularly hectic moment, just the week before. I felt it necessary to mention this. Otherwise, my conscience would have been seared with the image of her poor mother agonizing over a thank-you note received for a pin she couldn't remember buying or giving. No, Mom, it's we overloaded younger ones with the problem here!

Another friend said to me, only last night, that the mountain of stress she's going through has really taken its toll on her mind. "I'm usually only operating on about three-and-a-half out of eight cylinders anyway, but the way life is going lately, I think I only have the use of one." Or maybe she said two. I'm not sure because there were only the two of us having that conversation.

These stressful stages of our lives can be frustrating. And even though we laugh about it, we can be truly fearful at times. "What if I'm really losing it? I've actually looked at a friend I've known for years, and suddenly her name was just . . . gone!"

How do we adjust to the lapses? How do we cope with the thorns of limitations, failings, and decline in this world?

By honestly sharing the fears, the laughter, and the understanding acceptance that right now things just are as they are. By slowing down and resting. By simplifying. By choosing to enjoy together the sweet honey of God's renewing presence, power, hope, and encouragement. And it might help to wear a name tag so we won't forget who we are.

Whatever names we forget, we need to help one another remember His name, for there is peace and power nowhere else!

Be careful that you do not forget the LORD... *Deuteronomy* 6:12

For he knows how we are formed, he remembers that we are dust.
                                                    Psalm 103:14

The LORD *comforts his people and will have compassion on his afflicted ones. . . . "Can a mother forget the baby at her breast and have no compassion on the child she has borne? Though she may forget, I will not forget you!"   Isaiah* 49:13, 15

Let us not give up meeting together, as some are in the habit of doing, but let us encourage one another—and all the more as you see the Day approaching.   Hebrews 10:25

As iron sharpens iron, so one man [woman] sharpens another.
                                                    Proverbs 27:17

But one thing I do: Forgetting what is behind and straining toward what is ahead, I press on toward the goal to win the prize for which God has called me heavenward in Christ Jesus. All of us who are mature should take such a view of things. Philippians 3:13—15

What a Name!

A NAME, WHEN USED IN THE BIBLE, IS NOT
MERELY A DESIGNATION; IT IS A DEFINITION.
GOD'S NAMES REVEAL CERTAIN CHARACTERIS-
TICS WHICH ARE DISCLOSED ONLY WHEN HIS
PEOPLE ENTER AN AREA OF SPECIAL NEED.

SELWYN HUGHES

LET THEM PRAISE YOUR GREAT AND AWESOME
NAME.   PSALM 99:3

You wrote Your glorious name
across the heavens and it read
  Elohim—The Creator
You pronounced Your holy name
 to Your people and it was
  Yahweh—Lord of Relationship.
You posted Your powerful name
 at life's valleys and dead-ends and it was
  El Shaddai—All Sufficient God.
You spoke Your lovely name
 into fears and conflicts and it was
  Jehovah Shalom—The Lord Our Peace.
You whispered Your compassionate name
 into sorrow and brokenness and it was

Jehovah Jireh—The Lord Provides.
You signed Your most beautiful name
in blood upon our hearts and it was
Jesus—Jehovah is Salvation.

The name of the LORD is a strong tower; the righteous run to it
and are safe.   *Proverbs 18:10*

And everyone who calls on the name of the Lord will be saved.
                                                     Acts 2:21

Therefore God exalted him to the highest place and gave him the
name that is above every name, that at the name of Jesus every
knee should bow, in heaven and on earth and under the earth,
and every tongue confess that Jesus Christ is Lord, to the glory
of God the Father.   *Philippians 2:9–11*

Let the name of the LORD be praised, both now and forevermore.
From the rising of the sun to the place where it sets, the name of the
LORD is to be praised. The LORD is exalted over all the nations,
his glory above the heavens. Who is like the LORD our God, the
One who sits enthroned on high, who stoops down to look on the
heavens and the earth? He raises the poor from the dust and lifts
the needy from the ash heap; he seats them with princes, with the
princes of their people. He settles the barren woman in her home as
a happy mother of children. Praise the LORD.   *Psalm 113:2–9*

Rem✿ve This Th✿rn!

THERE WAS GIVEN ME A THORN IN MY
FLESH. . . . THREE TIMES I PLEADED WITH THE
LORD TO TAKE IT AWAY FROM ME.
                    PAUL, 2 CORINTHIANS 12:7–8

SOMETIMES I wonder if the apostle Paul tried to give tweezers to the Lord as he pleaded with Him to remove the thorn that was tormenting him. I probably would have.

We don't know exactly what the apostle's "thorn" was—perhaps a vision problem—but we do know that Paul was no sissy. If he was begging, it was bad. Still, God didn't take it away.

God answered, "My grace is sufficient to sustain you, Paul. I'll never hold a thorn to your side without supplying enough sweet grace to enable you to bear it." Not the answer he was hoping for. Me either.

And Paul was a special friend of God's, an incredibly tireless and faithful servant. I wonder if people told him he had sin in his life, or lacked faith?

We don't know the reason God refused to remove it any more than we know for certain what it was, or all that God accomplished through it. We do know that it was a place where God applied the ointment of His grace. And we know that it kept Paul humble and relying on the Lord for strength.

Who wants the constant stab of something that we believe

is hindering our work for the Lord, maybe even threatening our life? Something that has the power to distract, humble, and way-lay us? Persistent pain and problems—of whatever variety—sap energy, demand attention, and churn up doubts and fear.

I told the Lord I'd like to avoid dealing with the thorny issue of such pain, but He wouldn't let me get away with that. Because He is Truth and I am His servant. So I have to tell it like it is, even if writing about a God who deliberately holds us in a place of pain is unpopular with everyone, including me. We don't want to accept the idea of a heavenly Father who uses such a com-modity. It's hard to "give away" a God like that, and sometimes hard to keep Him, too.

One of the most important and difficult tasks God has given me in life, and in this book, is to face, and to help oth-ers face, the reality of who He is. He really is love! He really is good. And He really does deal in pain in this world. And I really don't like it.

Sometimes He removes and heals pain. Sometimes He per-mits and accomplishes things through it. Sometimes He even sends it. How unpopular is that last truth? When we want to avoid certain truths, we tend to label them "unscriptural." But I can't read the Scriptures without running into all three of these truths over and over. God uses this world's hurts, even though they don't originate in Him.

Pain is an arrow that Satan hurls and that God grabs, bends, and sends to His righteous purpose. But He ran it through His own heart first, so it comes dripping with the life-giving blood of His grace and love. God's purpose is that everyone should come to fully know Him, and live in His eternal love and joy in a place forever without sorrow and hurt. Not a single thorn in heaven.

What an amazing God we serve, who will use pain to get us to a place forever free of it! We don't have to understand or like the way it works. We just have to trust Him, submit to Him, and thank Him. It helps to remember the apostle Paul's words from prison, "I know that . . . what has happened to me will turn out for my deliverance" (Philippians 1:19).

We are also encouraged by Joseph's words to his brothers who had thrown him into a well and sold him into slavery in Egypt. "You intended to harm me," Joseph said, "but God intended it for good to accomplish what is now being done, the saving of many lives" (Genesis 50:20).

But it's not easy for us, any more than it is easy for our heavenly Father, when we must go through painful things.

When a parent must hold down a beloved child to receive chemotherapy or radiation, it is not so that the little one can suffer, but so that the child can live. The child can hear the parent's words, "Oh, Darling, you must go through this so you can have a chance to get well. Trust me. I know it's hard—I know it hurts—I know you hate it! I do too! But we have to go through this so you can be well and strong again. I love you so much, I can't bear to lose you. I want to keep you with me. I want you to grow up and become all you were meant to be, and do all you were meant to do—even better things than you can imagine yet. I want you to be able to get married and have your own children someday. I want you to laugh, and love, and do great things for the world. If you let me help you go through this, perhaps you can do all that someday. This won't last forever. I'm here my dear one. I'm here. I love you so much. Hold on! It will be better one day. So much better."

The child hears the words, but doesn't fully understand.

Someday, though, the child will understand, and will thank the parent for doing what was so very hard to do, bearing what was so hard to bear so that the child could live.

Someday we, too, will understand and thank our heavenly Father. It's safe to begin thanking Him now because although human cures sometimes fail, God's cure never does.

The principle of chemotherapy creates an interesting analogy for us. Chemotherapy poisons the entire system in an effort to destroy the deadly cancerous cells. That's why it makes people so ill. The doctor must be wise and good, and the person must be strong and brave to endure this cure which often works to make way for life in place of death. It may not be the treatment of choice if the cancer is localized, but it is often necessary when the entire system is permeated with cancer. Spot radiation won't do in this case.

This world of ours has cancer. The world's entire system has been permeated with deadly, multiplying sin. A single cancerous cell of rebellion has gone out of control, as both sin and cancer do. Sin has metastasized in this world. Only Jesus was strong enough to endure the cure for such a consuming sickness. He chose to let our sin produce death for His body. Then He produced life and healing for us as He conquered death.

This world is in its final declining stage with sin's cancer, but God will not give up on His rescue effort. In great mercy He is increasing His effort to save His dying children. Sometimes we may have to experience some of the pain. He chose not to take us out of this world, but prayed that the Father would keep us safe within it as He uses us in His salvation plan.

If God asks me to suffer because I'm in close proximity to cancer cells that are killing His beloved children, dare I say,

"Stop the treatment! This is hurting me too!"? I might want to, but I can't say that.

Dear Lord, give us grace to endure what You call us to endure for the sake of Your kingdom, no matter how much it hurts. We cannot help but love a God who gives Himself to save the dying sons and daughters of Adam and Eve.

> *The Spirit himself testifies with our spirit that we are God's children. Now if we are children, then we are heirs—heirs of God and co-heirs with Christ, if indeed we share in his sufferings in order that we may also share in his glory.*
>
> *I consider that our present sufferings are not worth comparing with the glory that will be revealed in us. The creation waits in eager expectation for the sons of God to be revealed. For the creation was subjected to frustration, not by its own choice, but by the will of the one who subjected it, in hope that the creation itself will be liberated from its bondage to decay and brought into the glorious freedom of the children of God.*
>
> *We know that the whole creation has been groaning as in the pains of childbirth right up to the present time. Not only so, but we ourselves, who have the firstfruits of the Spirit, groan inwardly as we wait eagerly for our adoption as sons, the redemption of our bodies. For in this hope we were saved.*
>
> *Romans 8:16—24*

Not What You Wanted

"MY THOUGHTS ARE NOT YOUR THOUGHTS,
NEITHER ARE YOUR WAYS MY WAYS," DECLARES
THE LORD. "AS THE HEAVENS ARE HIGHER
THAN THE EARTH, SO ARE MY WAYS HIGHER
THAN YOUR WAYS AND MY THOUGHTS THAN
YOUR THOUGHTS."   ISAIAH 55:8–9

JESUS' bewildered disciples watched in fear and disbelief as this Master they had followed, loved, and trusted for three years willingly walked into a situation where He was lied about, tortured, and hammered onto a cross to die. It was horrifying. Mind-boggling. It simply couldn't be right. Surely there must be some mistake. He had said He was God, yet there He hung, dying in agony!

This was not at all what they were expecting from Him.

This was not at all what they wanted.

This was not at all what they hoped for.

But it was what they needed. Their hope for eternal life depended upon it.

Is there something in your life right now that is not what you were expecting from God?

Not what you wanted, or hoped for at all?

Do you think God can produce eternal good through it anyway—no matter how awful it is?

He has a very good track record with that sort of thing, you know.

Jesus replied, "The hour has come for the Son of Man to be glorified. I tell you the truth, unless a kernel of wheat falls to the ground and dies, it remains only a single seed. But if it dies, it produces many seeds. The man who loves his life will lose it, while the man who hates his life in this world will keep it for eternal life. Whoever serves me must follow me; and where I am, my servant also will be. My Father will honor the one who serves me.

"Now my heart is troubled, and what shall I say? 'Father, save me from this hour'? No, it was for this very reason I came to this hour. Father, glorify your name!"

Then a voice came from heaven, "I have glorified it, and will glorify it again." John 12:23–28

Life's Confusing Caves

SOMETIMES A CAVE IS GOD'S CORRIDOR TO
THE FUTURE.   SL

YOU can't figure out what's going on. Everywhere you go and everything you do seems to deliver nothing but pressure and pain. You're not harboring unconfessed sin in your life, or creating your own problems with foolish choices, so what's happening?

You desperately hang onto the truth that God is good and delivers what He promises. Yet where are the promised blessings? Where are the victories? Why has God been permitting people and circumstances to harass and hem you in like this? You just want to run away and hide.

Join David in the cave of Adullam, the dark hiding place of a man who was promised a throne but was crowned with nothing but problems. No throne in sight.

One might logically assume that when God places a specific call on a person's life, that person would not be left to wait and wonder and wander around for years, struggling with circumstances that lead everywhere else. But that's exactly what happened to David. (See 1 Samuel 16–31 for the whole story.)

Several miserable years had passed since this surprised young man had been called in from the field, where he was contentedly tending his father's sheep, to face the prophet Samuel. Samuel pronounced that God had chosen David to replace Saul as King of Israel, and he promptly anointed the young boy with oil. Wow! Time to trade in his field clothes for royal robes.

Not quite. He entered the palace scene with a harp, not a scepter. Court musician. The songs he'd written under the stars to calm restless sheep, were now needed to sooth the agitated and tormented King Saul.

Other kingly duties? Slingshot detail. With a stone and his trusty slingshot, he felled a nine-foot giant named Goliath, who had been intimidating the entire army of Israel. He went to war, racking up huge military victories as he repeatedly slaughtered thousands of Israel's enemies. A blood-soaked battlefield instead of a palace?

In payment, the insecure and jealous king decided that his faithful servant was a threat to him, so he began trying to kill him. David had to run for his life. He ended up in the Philistine town of Gath, not the safest place for him since he had killed his share of Philistines in his military endeavors. Someone recognized him, and to save his own life, David had to carry on like a madman, pawing on the gates and letting saliva run down his beard.

This is when David escaped to the cave of Adullam, spit drying in his beard, undoubtedly confused, and desperately in need of someone to comfort him. So who does God send to his cave?

His brothers! Those same sweet siblings who mocked him at the battlefront when he stepped forward to slay Goliath. "Why have you come down here?" his oldest brother had asked haughtily. "And with whom did you leave those few sheep in the desert? I know how conceited you are and how wicked your heart is; you came down only to watch the battle" (1 Samuel 17:28).

Nice family. So glad to have you in my cave.

Next David is joined by hundreds of society's distressed,

debt-ridden, and discontented. Not exactly the kind of company I hope for when I run away.

In addition to all of this, David was trying to find a safe place for his aging mother and father to stay during his cave tenure. He really needed to get them taken care of because "he didn't know what God would do for him" (1 Samuel 22:3). Small wonder that he wondered—this anointed king whose throne was a stone, whose palace was a cave, and whose kingdom was a gang of society's disgruntled rejects.

So why this miserable cave scene? Was David being punished for something? Had he made some wrong choices? Did he have a bad attitude? There's nothing in his life so far to suggest that this was so.

There's everything to suggest that the fulfillment of God's highest and best promises come at the end of a path of pain. Perhaps it is the pain that prepares and purifies us. No one wants to believe that this is God's way. We don't want to remember that it was the cross and the cave—Christ's temporary grave— that led the way to resurrection and eternal, abundant life.

We prefer to blame it all on the enemy. We whine as if the devil has gotten by with some sneak attack when God wasn't looking. Or else we blame it on that poor person who is already suffering, who "must be doing something wrong or she wouldn't be going through all this."

We forget that Jesus promised we would have trouble in this world. In fact, He said that we *may* have peace (a choice, an available possibility), but we *will* have trouble (no choice, an absolute certainty) (John 16:33). Yes, sometimes we'll have trouble even when we're doing what's right. He asked us to take heart in the fact that He has overcome the world. He is practiced at turning the enemy's tricks to His own good purposes.

But while God works things out, we might find it necessary to "hide away for awhile." Escape or protection is sometimes appropriate, as it was for David in the cave of Adullum.

Yet even then, we may find God allowing what looks like more trouble to follow us into our caves. This may well become the stuff of our strength. Those four hundred malcontents who gathered with David became the power base that would sustain him throughout his later years as king— his most faithful men. Had he rejected them as just another unwelcome stress in his life, he would have missed the beginning of God's blessing for him. He went into the cave alone, but he came out leading warriors.

We use our cave times to rest—to learn—to grow—to prepare— to receive all that God has for us. So even if life doesn't get better, we get better at living it. Take heart. We will yet reign with Him!

Your granite cave a hiding place,
Your high cliff aerie a place of safety.
You're my cave to hide in,
my cliff to climb.
Be my safe leader,
be my true mountain guide.
Free me from hidden traps;
I want to hide in you.
I've put my life in your hands.
You won't drop me,
You'll never let me down.   Psalm 31:2–5 The Message

Have mercy on me, O God, have mercy on me, for in you my soul takes refuge. I will take refuge in the shadow of your wings until the disaster has passed.

I cry out to God Most High, to God, who fulfills his purpose for me. He sends from heaven and saves me, rebuking those who hotly pursue me; God sends his love and his faithfulness.

I am in the midst of lions; I lie among ravenous beasts—men whose teeth are spears and arrows, whose tongues are sharp swords.

Be exalted, O God, above the heavens; let your glory be over all the earth.

They spread a net for my feet—I was bowed down in distress. They dug a pit in my path—but they have fallen into it themselves.

My heart is steadfast, O God, my heart is steadfast; I will sing and make music. Awake, my soul! Awake, harp and lyre! I will awaken the dawn.

I will praise you, O Lord, among the nations; I will sing of you among the peoples. For great is your love, reaching to the heavens; your faithfulness reaches to the skies.

Be exalted, O God, above the heavens; let your glory be over all the earth.

David, from the cave where he fled from Saul
Psalm 57:1–11

Rejoice, My Soul!

BRING JOY TO YOUR SERVANT, FOR TO YOU,
O LORD, I LIFT UP MY SOUL.
                    KING DAVID, PSALM 86:4

I LOVE the way the Psalmist would have heart-to-heart talks with himself—especially when he was upset about something.

Can't you almost see David tugging his shirt open with both hands, lowering his chin into his collar and saying, "Hey, down there! What's your problem? Why are you so disturbed? Where did all your joy go?"

I don't know if his soul actually answered him or not, but he often proceeded to ask a lot of questions or make a lot of statements designed to change his emotional and spiritual landscape. He seemed to know how to work his way back to the joy every time it deserted him. We would do well to take lessons at his feet, because joy is as essential to us as air and water.

Joy is our eternal birthright as God's dearly loved children, and He means for it to begin now. Joy is life's bubbles, its song, and often its medicine. Joy knows how to lift our burdens and carry us over the rough spots in life.

And the joy of the Lord cannot, we soon discover, be kept cooped up inside us. It much prefers to come out to play in laughter, smiles, songs, dancing, praise, and endless kind words and actions. Soon joy becomes a "people magnet," drawing others into its warmth and light. God's joy is a party—a banquet—and everyone is invited.

Joy is our soul expressing its wonder in who and what God is, and joy increases as He increases. Joy is the dance of the redeemed. Joy is life, speaking back to Life, our gratitude.

Joy shouts to my soul, "Go ahead and dance on the dung-heap; you already know the outcome! You've already sampled the eternal good fruit God grows from this world's fertilizer. So go ahead and trust! Sing! Dance in the midst!"

But mired feet can't dance. Joy is difficult to find in the muck. Sometimes life even suggests that joy is inappropriate. And when we do find it, we can't always keep it. This world's thorns poke holes in our fragile containers, allowing our joy to leak.

When this happened to David, he acknowledged the problem, then set about addressing it within himself. He didn't pretend that if he were a truly godly man, or a truly successful servant of the Most High God, he would never feel upset, frightened, discouraged, deserted, ashamed, or depressed. He never pretended that he was experiencing joy when he wasn't. He simply asked himself what had taken the place of his joy, and began dealing with it.

He reminded himself of God's great love and goodness. He revived his perspective, renewed his trust, rekindled his hope, restored his relationship, and ultimately received once more the joy of the Lord. I especially love the way he then spread it around, inviting every living thing in heaven and on earth to join in the party of praise.

You and I also have the privilege of inviting men and angels to rejoice. But first we need to invite our own soul to sing.

Why are you downcast, O my soul? Why so disturbed within me? Put your hope in God, for I will yet praise him, my Savior and my God. My soul is downcast within me; therefore I will remember you.   Psalm 42:5—6

Find rest, O my soul, in God alone; my hope comes from him.
He alone is my rock and my salvation; he is my fortress, I will
not be shaken.   Psalm 62:5–6

When anxiety was great within me, your consolation brought
joy to my soul.   Psalm 94:19

Praise the Lord, O my soul; all my inmost being, praise his
holy name. Praise the Lord, O my soul, and forget not all his
benefits—who forgives all your sins and heals all your diseases,
who redeems your life from the pit and crowns you with love and
compassion, who satisfies your desires with good things so that
your youth is renewed like the eagle's.
     Praise the Lord, you his angels, you mighty ones who do his
bidding, who obey his word. Praise the Lord, all his heavenly
hosts, you his servants who do his will. Praise the Lord, all his
works everywhere in his dominion.
     Praise the Lord, O my soul.   Psalm 103:1–5; 20–22

Thorny Little Issues

CATCH FOR US THE FOXES, THE LITTLE FOXES
THAT RUIN THE VINEYARDS.
SONG OF SONGS 2:15

I DON'T have a cat or dog in my life, but I've been known to have a pet peeve or two to keep me company. Surely I'm not the only one who has thorny little irritants and vexations that nibble at happiness and act as gauges to reveal my levels of tolerance and patience at any given moment.

You might even be dealing with one of my favorite pet peeves of days gone by—the "Rapture practice scene"—the collapsed pile of clothes on the bedroom floor that looks as if the person wearing them had suddenly been vaporized. In hope of a solution, you settle for open hampers without those complicated lids to lift. The piles of clothes minus the people continue.

But these kinds of irritations have left home now, so I find other things to ruin my happiness. Things like drivers who suddenly change lanes in front of me without even having the common courtesy to flip on a simple turn signal. (Apparently those levers must be as tricky as hamper lids!) What do they think that knob is there for anyway, could they just answer me that?

And then there are those phone calls (I really hate this one!) that you run to grab, breathless and covered with paint or dirt, or worse, because you're expecting an important call. And then it turns out to be a total stranger trying to sell something—usually by claiming they're "not selling anything!" Or worse, it's a tape recorder that somehow dialed your phone to announce that you—lucky you!—have been selected for something that's such a rare privilege it takes a mass auto-dialing to distribute all the good fortune. And now you can't seem to disconnect from this stroke of good luck. Don't you just hate that?

One recording even impersonated a friend. As soon as I said hello, it responded in a casual voice saying, "Oh good! I caught you home!" so that I actually found myself speaking with kindness to a recording. Can you believe it? I talked nicely to a stupid, inanimate, machine that just kept babbling while I spoke! How embarrassing is that?

People today are laboring under a lot of new frustrations in our fast-paced world. Exasperating new issues are multiplying at DSL speed. (Don't let me even get started on my computer complaints!)

So, are we required to find God's honey in the midst of these ever-present prickers and stickers? It seems easier to deal with the big stuff than with the daily nonsense. Irritation over the intrusiveness of technology and total strangers seems justified and somehow part of our allowance for living in this annoying world. But it's not. We need to admit that.

Truly it is the "little foxes that ruin the vine." And they get away with it because we allow them entrance to our vineyard. We feed them. Make pets of them.

Both my attitude and my days will be sweeter when I remember to pray for the people creating the problem rather than protesting them. God loves the nameless driver behind the wheel of that other car and that faceless stranger on the phone. These are not faceless and nameless annoyances to Him. They are beloved people made in His image. I need to stop and remember that He knows and loves the person whose voice is on that automated recording, and the one who operates such an intrusive business. He requires me to love them, too.

If I had prayed each time these people intruded into my world, asking God to draw them to Himself and bless them, I would have lost a few pet peeves and gained some peace and joy. I have a feeling He'll give me a few more "opportunities" to get it right.

"If someone takes unfair advantage of you, use the occasion to practice the servant life. No more tit-for-tat stuff. Live generously.

"You're familiar with the old written law, 'Love your friend,' and its unwritten companion, 'Hate your enemy.' I'm challenging that. I'm telling you to love your enemies. Let them bring out the best in you, not the worst. When someone gives you a hard time, respond with the energies of prayers, for then you are working out of your true selves, your God-created selves. This is what God does. He gives his best—the sun to warm and the rain to nourish—to everyone, regardless: the good and bad, the nice and nasty. If all you do is love the lovable, do you expect a bonus? Anybody can do that. If you simply say hello to those who greet you, do you expect a medal? Any run-of-the-mill sinner does that.

"In a word, what I'm saying is, Grow up. You're kingdom subjects. Now live like it. Live out of your God-created identity. Live generously and graciously toward others, the way God lives toward you." Jesus, Matthew 5:41–48 The Message

Praying Over the Family Album

IF REGRET OVER THE PAST LEADS US TO
PRAYER IN THE PRESENT, THEN THE FUTURE
WILL BE CHANGED.   SL

Wisdom seen too late weighs heavy, Lord.
I've been leafing through my costly album of
perfectly framed family portraits.
See us gathered and smiling around the festive table.
Here we're posed and pretty beside the blazing hearth.
Yet I wonder . . . are my children's memory books
littered with the stressful scenes surrounding such
perfectly constructed moments?
Did I think idealism, enlarged and framed,
would somehow cover such painful memories?
Oh Lord, unbound by past and present—
Compassionate One, who said,
"Before they call I will answer,"—
hear this prayer as from the lips of a young mother,
but crafted in the heart of an older, wiser one.
The memories I would leave them are of
baking and cleaning up the kitchen together,
not just eating the cookies on Christmas—
of the real, framed with patience,
not the ideal, framed with perfection.
Please transcend time in their hearts.

Godly sorrow brings repentance that leads to salvation and leaves no regret, but worldly sorrow brings death. 2 Corinthians 7:10

Yet I am not ashamed, because I know whom I have believed, and am convinced that he is able to guard what I have entrusted to him for that day. . . . Guard the good deposit that was entrusted to you—guard it with the help of the Holy Spirit who lives in us.

2 Timothy 1:12, 14

Commit to the LORD *whatever you do, and your plans will succeed. The* LORD *works out everything for his own ends.*

Proverbs 16:3—4

Deflated Dreams

NOTHING WOUNDS US MORE DEEPLY THAN
RUNNING FROM THE TRUTH, EVEN WHEN
TRUTH HURTS.   SL

SOME people have a lot of wrinkled little rubber balloons of "expectations" and "hopes" lying around inside of them. They fear and avoid these deflated dreams, as though honest acknowledgment might inflate them until they explode.

Honestly facing life's disappointments can be painful. It can even seem like the ultimate disappointment. We would rather believe that if we don't look at or admit the truth, then maybe it's not real, or it doesn't matter so much after all.

"How can I admit that life stinks? That it's not turning out right? That the very people and things I most wanted to be proud of—had the highest dreams and hopes for—have deeply disappointed me? That the grand plan I had for life has been derailed? That even some of the goals that I did reach are lying on the floor too, empty of the satisfaction I thought they would bring? Why would I admit this? It sounds like an invitation to depression to me!"

No, it's an invitation to avoid depression. Buried feelings of disappointment gang up inside us and whisper lies in the dark about who we are, whose fault it is, or what the future holds. Buried disappointments believe the lies of fear and failure, and avoid the truth that would set us free. Disappointments that are brought into God's light meet His hope and resurrection power.

I think the enemy takes advantage of these hopes, dreams, and intentions that have fallen short or just exploded. I think he tries to apply them to the hope that we have in God, causing us to begin to lower our expectations of God, transferring the reality of a life that disappoints on some levels, to a God that disappoints on some levels.

But it's not God's fault. Sometimes I think about how disappointed our heavenly Father must be in the choices of His children. Parents who watch their own children make harmful choices that divert them from the path to becoming all they could be, can relate to what our Lord must be feeling.

If you are a parent grieving for your child who seems lost and derailed from God's highest intentions, know that the Father enters into your disappointment with you. He will share with that deepest aching part of your "Mother or Father heart" the reality and joy that He has not given up hope, therefore you must not either. Because He "knows Himself"—He knows who He is, and what He can do. He knows the powerful resources of His great love. If He can give life to the dead, He can surely give abundant purposeful life to the living.

Our heavenly Father truly knows all that we could be, should be, and were created to be. He doesn't know this as some vague "hope" but as reality. How it must have hurt Him to give up this reality for the lie we bought! Oh, the high intentions He had, and has, for us! Yet here we are, charting our own course and trying to pretend it doesn't matter that we aren't getting there.

Still, God enters into our "lousy choice situations" and continues giving in order to help us survive and grow in the midst of it. He longs and waits for us to become who and what He intended. Yet many of us take advantage of His grace, love, and patience for our own selfish and shortsighted gain, rather than take advantage of His grace and love to become like Him in selfless, sacrificial love. Selfishness and blindness run deep in our fallen, human condition.

Courage, dear one! God simply ain't done yet! The final chapter hasn't been written. Well, it's actually written, but we just haven't read it yet. Maybe faith and hope mean nothing more than peeking at the end of the book—reading the invisible pages through passages like 2 Corinthians 4:16–18, and Romans 8:15–39, and then getting excited and living in gratitude and joy about what He's doing. No matter what it looks like right now.

But I think this comes about only when we look at the pain honestly and weep over it. Sometimes I think we have to get the tears out to make more room for the hope and joy.

You'll know you've traded in your disappointments and deflated dreams for faith and hope when you find yourself being filled with the knowledge that God will yet change hearts and open blind eyes. And you'll really know that faith is afloat when you catch yourself praying that your child, spouse, or friend won't kick his or her back-side all the way through the front-side in regret for not "getting it" sooner!

Keep loving, dear one. Keep hoping in God. I believe in Him, and I believe in you.

May the God of hope fill you with all joy and peace as you trust in him, so that you may overflow with hope by the power of the Holy Spirit.   Romans 15:13

Facing Reality

BUT WHOEVER LIVES BY THE TRUTH COMES
INTO THE LIGHT.   JOHN, JOHN 3:21

I tried to pretend
but the truth wanted in.
I tried to deny
but was living a lie.
I kept running away,
but there came the day
when I fell on my face,
and in that prone place
where pain and truth meet
I lifted my eyes and saw nail-scarred feet.

*This is good, and pleases God our Savior, who wants all men to
be saved and to come to a knowledge of the truth.* 1 Timothy 2:3

*I have no greater joy than to hear that my children are walking
in the truth.*   3 John 4

Root of the Problem

MY computer gave me an interesting tip today. It dropped a little dialog box onto my screen announcing, "Things that go away by themselves can come back by themselves."

"Hmmm," said my right brain.

"Wait a minute now," said my left brain. "Considering the source, this clearly was meant to suggest that you shouldn't just ignore a computer problem until it goes away. You need to discover what's amiss in the system and deal with it before it comes back and gets you good—or, more likely, gets you bad."

But with me, right brain reigns. Technical tips are seldom read with a "technical" eye. I'm not sure I even own that kind of an "eye." Everything and anything can suggest an analogy or some deeper meaning. This statement went there all by itself.

It reminded me that denial and avoidance are great Band-Aids for life's annoyances. And sometimes things do seem to go away when we ignore them.

Herb used to have a theory about things in need of repair. It went like this: If you leave it alone long enough, it will heal itself. This theory was frequently applied to our appliances and cars. To my constant amazement, and considerable annoyance, it occasionally worked. At least for a while. But when a thing is truly faulty, it can't go on long in the way it was designed to operate. Someone who understands the system has to deal with the source of the problem.

God understands the system. He didn't ignore or patch over our sin problem. He dealt with it once and for all through Jesus Christ. And He asks each of us to deal with our sin condition once and for all as we accept this gift of forgiveness and new life.

But there are still certain sins that pierce us daily. Those thorns of wrong choices and wrong thinking that bury themselves in our flesh and fester. How it must grieve God when we rationalize, "It's just a small sliver; it will go away."

If the invading infection inhibits our ability to move forward, we may borrow a crutch from a friend and keep going. We take vitamins— more prayer and Bible study—and hope that will take care of it.

If the infected area gets really uncomfortable, we swipe some antiseptic ointment across it—"God knows I'm not perfect! Anyway, He doesn't even see this. After all, I wear the righteousness of Christ, don't I?" And we insult Him by taking one of His precious promises and making of it a Band-Aid to cover the mess.

Sometimes a friend will dress the contaminated site for us, suggesting it's just a flaw or something from our past that we have no control over. They assure us it will go away as we mature.

We are skilled at finding alternate remedies to God's command to cleanly lance our festering sin with the honest confession that removes the offense. As C. S. Lewis said, "Conditions are not causes." We need to name the cause of our problem.

It's important to uncover those deep hidden places because only uncovered sins are truly covered.

If we confess our sins, he is faithful and just to forgive us our sins, and to cleanse us from all unrighteousness.   1 John 1:9 NKJV

Therefore confess your sins to each other and pray for each other so that you may be healed.   James 5:16

Field of Dreams

THE KINGDOM OF HEAVEN IS LIKE TREASURE
HIDDEN IN A FIELD. WHEN A MAN FOUND IT,
HE HID IT AGAIN, AND THEN IN HIS JOY WENT
AND SOLD ALL HE HAD AND BOUGHT THAT
FIELD.   JESUS, MATTHEW 13:44

*I wish that I could say
I sold my all and
shrewdly
bought that field
which hid the
Greatest of all
treasures.
Instead I gaze with tears
upon my tiny plot of
ruined earth;
where at my feet,
in ashes, gleams
The Pearl of Great Price,
Who sold Himself to
purchase me.*

*It wasn't so long ago that you were mired in that old stagnant
life of sin. You let the world, which doesn't know the first thing
about living, tell you how to live. You filled your lungs with*

polluted unbelief, and then exhaled disobedience. We all did it, all of us doing what we felt like doing, when we felt like doing it, all of us in the same boat. It's a wonder God didn't lose his temper and do away with the whole lot of us. Instead, immense in mercy and with an incredible love, he embraced us. He took our sin-dead lives and made us alive in Christ. He did all this on his own, with no help from us! Then he picked us up and set us down in highest heaven in company with Jesus, our Messiah.

Now God has us where he wants us, with all the time in this world and the next to shower grace and kindness upon us in Christ Jesus. Saving is all his idea, and all his work. All we do is trust him enough to let him do it. It's God's gift from start to finish! We don't play the major role. If we did, we'd probably go around bragging that we'd done the whole thing! No, we neither make nor save ourselves. God does both the making and the saving. . . .

God can do anything, you know—far more than you could ever imagine or guess or request in your wildest dreams!

Ephesians 2:1–10; 3:20 The Message

Caught in Life's Brambles

LIKE FISH TAKEN IN A CRUEL NET, AND LIKE
BIRDS CAUGHT IN A SNARE, SO MORTALS ARE
SNARED AT A TIME OF CALAMITY, WHEN IT
SUDDENLY FALLS UPON THEM.

ECCLESIASTES 9:12 NRSV

Imprisoned one,
  caught up in
  fears and failures,
  hopelessly ensnared,
try to remember . . .
Discouraged one,
  entangled in life's
  pain and problems,
  thinking no one cares,
try to remember . . .
When you can't find the way,
you need to find The Way.
Jesus is still
  The Way
   The Truth
   The Life.
He was your Way in
and He is your Way out.
Escape into His freedom.
Do this in remembrance of Him.

Jesus answered, "I am the way and the truth and the life. No one comes to the Father except through me."   John 14:6

The Spirit of the Sovereign LORD is on me, because the LORD has anointed me to preach good news to the poor. He has sent me to bind up the brokenhearted, to proclaim freedom for the captives and release from darkness for the prisoners, to proclaim the year of the LORD's favor and the day of vengeance of our God, to comfort all who mourn, and provide for those who grieve in Zion—to bestow on them a crown of beauty instead of ashes, the oil of gladness instead of mourning, and a garment of praise instead of a spirit of despair.   Isaiah 61:1–3

Escaping the Briar Patch

LOVE IS THE ONLY RATIONAL ACT. LET IT
COME IN.   MORRIE SCHWARTZ

I WAS seeing important things. Hearing profound things. Witnessing deeply moving truths. And I was watching television. Hard to believe, I know. But I was watching the excellent made-for-television movie *Tuesdays with Morrie*, based on the book of the same name by Mitch Albom. I have to say, it was the worst best movie I ever saw. "Worst" because it was painful to see and it made me cry. "Best" because it was an honest, tender, and moving true story of the persevering power of genuine love that wins out in both life and death.

This is the story of Mitch Albom's many conversations with his former college professor and wise friend, Morrie Schwartz. Although Morrie was dying of ALS, he spent every Tuesday challenging this young friend with his lifetime of accumulated insights about living, loving, and dying.

At that time, Mitch was a sports writer trapped on the treadmill of this world's shallow success, trying to outrun his fears. Morrie helped him to face and find so much of what is truly important in life, and let go of what isn't. He helped him to overcome his resistance to letting love inside where it has the power to hurt, but also to enrich and change us. And just in time too, because he almost lost the beautiful love of his life, Janine, in his headlong race to nowhere important.

It turns out that excessive involvement with what passes for living can help us avoid a multitude of things we'd rather not stop and face—such as whether anything we're doing will really matter in the end.

Left to itself, life manages to get crowded and consuming. And that's simply with the good and necessary activities. But when we are trying to outrun our fears, needs, and inadequacies, or when we don't have our priorities straight, we often take on extra busyness as an escape, or to prove something to someone, or perhaps out of good but misguided intentions. And so we can miss what's truly important.

We need to escape this tangled briar patch of doing too much. We need to slow down. Even we who are working hard serving the Lord probably need to slow down. Why? Because any relationship requires time to grow and blossom. As followers of Christ we are, first and foremost, in a living and vital love relationship with Him. There is nothing I am doing—absolutely nothing—that's more important than spending time with Him.

> *Gratefully serving*
> *the One who saved me*
> *from sin's dark night.*
> *So busy going and*
> *giving and doing,*
> *trying with all my might.*
> *How did I miss Him,*
> *the Lover of my Soul,*
> *waiting with*
> *roses and candlelight and*
> *empty arms?*

"Come to me, all you who are weary and burdened, and I will give you rest. Take my yoke upon you and learn from me, for I am gentle and humble in heart, and you will find rest for your souls. For my yoke is easy and my burden is light."

Jesus, Matthew 11:28–30

May the favor of the Lord our God rest upon us; establish the work of our hands for us—yes, establish the work of our hands. . . .

He who dwells in the shelter of the Most High will rest in the shadow of the Almighty. I will say of the LORD, "He is my refuge and my fortress, my God, in whom I trust."

My soul finds rest in God alone; my salvation comes from him.

Psalm 90:17; 91:1–2; 62:1

Running from God

BE SURE OF THIS—THAT I AM WITH YOU
ALWAYS, EVEN TO THE END OF THE WORLD.
JESUS, MATTHEW 28:20 TLB

So, you're running away from God.
  Angry. Rebellious. Full of doubts.
Fearing the offense of disagreeing with Deity—
  fearing to question a God beyond question.
Is it possible God is more offended when we:
  imagine we can hide from
    omnipresence?
  Think His ear may be too fragile
    for our pain?
  Pretend He cannot hear our
    unvoiced anger?
  Deny our doubt can find its
    answer within Him?
  Decide that mercy cannot meet us
    where we are?
  Refuse the second chance He's
    offering right now?

Oh, how kind our Lord was, for he showed me how to trust him
and become full of the love of Christ Jesus.

How true it is, and how I long that everyone should know it, that Christ Jesus came into the world to save sinners—and I was the greatest of them all. But God had mercy on me so that Christ Jesus could use me as an example to show everyone how patient he is with even the worst sinners, so that others will realize that they, too, can have everlasting life. Glory and honor to God forever and ever. He is the King of the ages, the unseen one who never dies; he alone is God, and full of wisdom. Amen.

Paul, 1 Timothy 1:14–17 TLB

Letter from Jesus

THEY SWARMED AROUND ME LIKE BEES, BUT
THEY DIED OUT AS QUICKLY AS BURNING
THORNS; IN THE NAME OF THE LORD I CUT
THEM OFF.   PSALM 118:12

I HUNG up the phone after praying with a beloved one who had called, weeping in pain and frustration. As I lay the phone in its cradle a letter began to form in my mind. It was clear and urgent, and it was in the first person—"me," "my," and "I." But I knew it was not from me.

It seemed that the Lord wanted me to stop what I was doing and deliver a message to one of His most beloved hurting children. Deeply honored to be heaven's secretary, I typed and dared to send it "from God, via Susan."

Along with her husband, she read it tearfully and then phoned again, this time to express her gratitude. For which I was grateful; the letter was so direct and pointed at times, that I'd been concerned that she might be upset with me. But at the end of our conversation she commented that she could imagine this letter in one of my books someday. "You would allow me to do that?" I asked, amazed.

She would. She hopes it may help you, too. So with some personal details removed, here is a message to a child caught up in the kind of hurt that holds the soul hostage to anger and bitterness.

My Precious Hurting Child,

I know that you have experienced some terrible betrayals and stabbing wounds in this world. And I know that you are not just hurting; you are angry. Did you know that I am, too?

For one thing, I'm angry at the Evil One for lying to you about yourself and about Me, and getting you to believe it in the midst of your pain. He is such a thief! He has managed to rob you of the peace, joy, love, and hope I paid so much to give you as your new inheritance.

I hurt with the agony of your fear and mistrust. That liar has told you that you dare not trust Me with this—told you that if you rebel against Me you'll spare yourself the unthinkable pain of having to deal with and face this deep-rooted hurt and bitterness.

Yet the truth is, your unwillingness to surrender to Me is keeping you in this place of torment—actually binding you to it—holding you in the most intolerable place of misery imaginable. But I don't need to tell you that. You're there and you know it. You're almost frantic to escape. I hear your cries.

Oh, how I hate what sin has done to you and my other precious children! Please let Me help you. Let Me give you your new inheritance. Believe Me, I know about your earthly heritage—so much hurt and damage. Do you have any idea how deeply I love you and long to rescue you from this terrible place you're in—how much I want to give you what you need?

I hear you saying, "Well what's the problem then? Go ahead and give me what I need! After all, You're God, aren't You? So just give me the peace and love you clearly see that I need but don't have!"

The problem is that I have a clear view of your heart. And if you could see what I'm seeing you'd realize that there's simply no room there for the love or peace that comes with forgiveness. You are packed full of resentment and murderous anger. Your righteous feelings of outraged justice fill you with the conviction that hate and bitterness are actually appropriate and right under the circumstances.

And it is right to hate sin—right to be outraged by what it does—but I am the only One equipped to deal with sin without being eternally poisoned by it. I am the only One able to fully hate the sin yet fully love the sinner. I have already paid the price for its burial, and taken it from the cross to the grave! Give it to Me, dearest child. Let it go. Release. Forgive. Make room for Me, and I will love through you.

You have not hidden from Me the fact that your indignation and sense of justice would actually like Me to strike that troublemaker dead and remove the problem from you. But, precious one, don't you realize that even if I took this person away, the problem would not be gone? The problem lives in you and has become a part of who you are.

I promised that you would be a new creation in Me, and now I'm asking you to let Me keep My promise. Determine to be done with this caterpillar crawling through the dirt of resentment and retribution! I'm here to transform you and set you free to soar!

But, first, I need you to do something for Me. I need you to tell Me what you're so afraid of? I'm asking you to be completely honest, and I trust you to do that, because you do it so well. (I love that about you!)

Are you afraid that if you surrender to Me I'll keep

you in this intolerable situation? (Ask one of my experienced children, sometime, what I can do to change everything when the circumstance remains the same but the person has let Me change her.)

But perhaps that is precisely what you're afraid of. Are you afraid that I'll leave the situation unchanged and change your heart, giving you a heart of forgiveness and love? And you don't want to love, or even like, this person! You don't want it to be okay! You want me to fix them!

May I say, then, that your first job needs to be surrender of your "right" to be God and to define justice? Such justice is devoid of love and forgiveness—and where would you be today if My justice were the same? Justice without mercy is not who I am, or what I do. And it cannot be who you are, or what you do either, My child.

You have gulped My grace and mercy; now let it pass through you to others who don't deserve it but who need it just as desperately.

But I see another fear. You are afraid that if you lay down your "armor of anger" (and anger is Satan's armor!) you'll be vulnerable to more hurt. Tell Me, could vulnerability be worse than the pain you're in right now, hugging this bitterness to your soul? This bitter armor you wear to protect yourself and preserve your power and control, will kill you.

Lay it down—it's too heavy for you to bear. Let Me pick it up and bear it away. Then I will give you the full armor of God—the same armor I wore when I went naked to the cross. This armor is tested and guaranteed safe! Remember what I conquered wearing this invisible, invincible armor.

And remember that I'm with you always and love you passionately,

Jesus

And do not grieve the Holy Spirit of God, with whom you were sealed for the day of redemption. Get rid of all bitterness, rage and anger, brawling and slander, along with every form of malice. Be kind and compassionate to one another, forgiving each other, just as in Christ God forgave you.　Ephesians 4:30–32

Finally, be strong in the Lord and in his mighty power. Put on all of God's armor so that you will be able to stand safe against all strategies and tricks of Satan. For we are not fighting against people made of flesh and blood, but against persons without bodies—the evil rulers of the unseen world, those mighty satanic beings and great evil princes of darkness who rule this world; and against huge numbers of wicked spirits in the spirit world.

So use every piece of God's armor to resist the enemy whenever he attacks, and when it is all over, you will still be standing up.

But to do this, you will need the strong belt of truth and the breastplate of God's approval. Wear shoes that are able to speed you on as you preach the Good News of peace with God. In every battle you will need faith as your shield to stop the fiery arrows aimed at you by Satan. And you will need the helmet of salvation and the sword of the Spirit—which is the Word of God.

Pray all the time. Ask God for anything in line with the Holy Spirit's wishes. Plead with him, reminding him of your needs, and keep praying earnestly for all Christians everywhere.

Ephesians 6:11–18 TLB

The Power of Forgiveness

RESENTMENT IS LIKE DRINKING POISON AND
WAITING FOR THE OTHER PERSON TO DIE.
CARRIE FISHER

THE need for forgiveness follows us around in this world. Who can get through even one day without needing to give or receive it? Yet, ironically, when such grace is most urgently needed, it is often the hardest to give.

I have heard people say, "I can't forgive this. I just can't let go of it." And it breaks my heart to hear those words. Because what we can't let go of takes hold of us. Resentment and bitterness set in, for we have lashed ourselves to the pain, giving it eternal life within us.

"I cannot forgive," really means, "I will not forgive." But we don't want to see this. We are blinded by our deep injury and hemmed in by our personal sense of justice. Do we even notice when we're no longer grieving the shaft of loss that has pierced us, but are clutching and sharpening it into an arrow aimed at someone we hold responsible for our pain? Holding onto resentment is our way of holding the person accountable for the wrong done to us. It's our way of keeping our finger pointed at the guilty one—of making the person pay. Do we even notice how much it is costing us?

Forgiving seems wrong, somehow. Like condoning the offense. Like "letting the person off the hook." Like saying that the horrible, thoughtless, evil, irresponsible, or selfish thing the person said or did that created such pain doesn't really matter.

But that's not what forgiveness says at all. Forgiveness says that it *does* matter. And that is why the power and validation found in the act of forgiving are so needed.

Forgiveness acknowledges and accepts the reality and the consequences of another person's wrong, and then chooses to release the debt. No strings attached. This is what Jesus did and does for us.

Man's unrighteous and angry justice is a demand for personal revenge. God's righteous justice always has a cross in the middle of it—an undeserved cross that we must choose to bear before we can rise to the eternal vibrant life found in full forgiveness. To forgive is a position of strength, not of weakness. To forgive is an act of God, and a gift of God.

Dennis Baker once said, "Forgiving is not forgetting. It is remembering that the issue has been addressed and dealt with. It's letting go—moving on by following Christ as a forgiven one who is a forgiver who keeps on forgiving."

Indeed, this will be an ongoing battle. But God continually offers us the freedom of forgiveness, even while requiring that we follow His example and, in His strength, forgive over and over. For that's what love does.

As always, our God of love is waiting to lift us above the pain and to bring others along the moment we join Him in honestly saying, "You are forgiven."

"For if you forgive men when they sin against you, your heavenly Father will also forgive you. But if you do not forgive men their sins, your Father will not forgive your sins."
Jesus, Matthew 6:14–15

Bear with each other and forgive whatever grievances you may have against one another. Forgive as the Lord forgave you.

Colossians 3:13

Set Free to Soar

ONE DAY YOU WILL LOOK BACK ON YOUR
FORMER DETERMINATION TO STAY IN THE
DIRT AND WONDER HOW YOU RESISTED YOUR
FATHER'S KINDNESS FOR SO LONG AND AT
SUCH COST.   BRUCE WILKINSON

Dear Lord,
don't let me be a
butterfly ensnared in
binding but familiar ways.
Nor would I be a
bright winged thing who
hugs earth's dirt afraid of sky.
I give You all I hold that
holds me down
and keeps me bound.
Please set me fully free—
I want to fly!

[Jesus] is able to save completely those who come to God through
him, because he always lives to intercede for them.   Hebrews 7:25

It is for freedom that Christ has set us free.   Galatians 5:1

They will soar on wings like eagles. . . .   Isaiah 40:31

Living the Questions

IF TRUST AND LOVE REQUIRED FULL UNDER-
STANDING, CHILDREN WOULD NEVER LOVE
THEIR PARENTS.   SL

WHY do we want, and sometimes even demand, answers to the hard questions about life—those things that so wound and baffle us? What are we really asking when we badger God to tell us why He's allowing such painful things to happen?

"Why are children dying and killing one another?" "Why do we have disease and tragedy?" "Why is there betrayal and divorce?" "Why do we live with hate, cruelty, war, and destruction?" "Why are there earthquakes, floods, hurricanes?" "Why do even good people suffer?" "Why are You allowing me to suffer?" "Why are You allowing even this to be taken from me?"

Do our endless "why" questions suggest that we cannot, or will not, fully trust and love a God we cannot fully understand—a God who works in and through pain? Then surely we will never have the blessed peace of trusting and resting in Him on this earth. For even if He told us what we beg to know, our finite minds could not fully grasp our infinite God, or what He is accomplishing in us, and how, in the midst of this sin-riddled world.

Some people hold only a thin hope that God truly hears and answers prayers, or that His claims of being all-powerful and good are true. Some of these desperate people might be His own children who, day after day, live with their own tragedy and pain. Others listen to the evening news, trying to hide a growing suspicion that God is actually powerless against this world's evil. Their constant "why" questions demand that He prove Himself.

Despite the fact that sin is here by human choice, people who doubt God in their pain, refuse to fully embrace a God who claims a power over sin that He does not demonstrate by erasing evil and its consequences from our lives and world now. They fear serving a Jesus who seems to be ever standing before Pilate, whipped and beaten by wickedness, saying and doing nothing. Somehow His silent patience, then and now, is seen as impotence, or lack of love.

These dear ones miss the incredible power and love of our Almighty Creator with a bowed head, wearing our crown of thorns.

This is a God who could and can lash back, eradicating sin and the sinner so steeped in it. Instantly. Yet He is a God who chose, and yet chooses, to bow His head and take our thorns. He will not always stand this way with His arms held out.

One day He will say, "Enough. I am coming to put an end to sin, and take those home with Me who would believe and gratefully live in a love they could not fully understand. I will gather those who came to Me as little children, who did not measure their Father's love by the circumstances in which they were loved."

As we live through the final death throes of wickedness in this world, we are watching and learning that sin is still deadly, and redemption still costly. Our patient, gracious, and compassionate God still waits and rescues from the midst.

At last we think to ask Him, not why He is yet allowing so much pain—clearly it is still here because sin and consequences are still here—but rather, why He stands with us in it, rescuing still?

And finally we hear God's gentle question. "Why are you so slow to ask Me to use these painful thorns in your life as part of My redemption plan? It's one of the things I do best, you know."

We don't need to understand any more than we have already learned from the foot of the cross, and the mouth of the empty tomb. We need comfort and hope more than we need answers. When we allow God to provide that, we can live life's painful questions until He fully reveals His secret wisdom in that final day. With His strength, and in His love, we can wait with patient joy even in the midst of tears.

We speak of God's secret wisdom, a wisdom that has been hidden and that God destined for our glory before time began. None of the rulers of this age understood it, for if they had, they would not have crucified the Lord of glory. However, as it is written: "No eye has seen, no ear has heard, no mind has conceived what God has prepared for those who love him"—but God has revealed it to us by his Spirit.

The Spirit searches all things, even the deep things of God. . . .

"For who has known the mind of the Lord that he may instruct him?"

But we have the mind of Christ.   1 Corinthians 2:7–10, 16

We rejoice in the hope of the glory of God. Not only so, but we also rejoice in our sufferings, because we know that suffering produces perseverance; perseverance, character; and character, hope. And hope does not disappoint us, because God has poured out his love into our hearts by the Holy Spirit, whom he has given us.

Romans 5:2–5

Thorns Will Increase

DO NOT BE AFRAID OF WHAT YOU ARE ABOUT
TO SUFFER. . . . BE FAITHFUL, EVEN TO THE
POINT OF DEATH, AND I WILL GIVE YOU THE
CROWN OF LIFE.   REVELATION 2:10

Oh Christian,
kneel at Christ's feet as
evil ascends to power,
as arrogant men mock and lie and maim,
fists thrust into the face of the Almighty.
Do not be afraid.
Just stay at His nail-scarred feet and
praise Him as troubles mount,
as nation rises against nation and
our world seems to spiral out of control.
Wait patiently and pray,
for all that lifts itself up will
fall at the feet of this One you worship.
For He is Lord,
and every stiffened knee will one day
bow beside you.

"You will hear of wars and rumors of wars, but see to it that
you are not alarmed. Such things must happen, but the end

is still to come. Nation will rise against nation, and kingdom against kingdom. There will be famines and earthquakes in various places. All these are the beginning of birth pains.

"Then you will be handed over to be persecuted and put to death, and you will be hated by all nations because of me. At that time many will turn away from the faith and will betray and hate each other, and many false prophets will appear and deceive many people. Because of the increase of wickedness, the love of most will grow cold, but he who stands firm to the end will be saved."

Jesus, Matthew 24:6–13

"As surely as I live," says the Lord, "every knee will bow before me; every tongue will confess to God."

So then, each of us will give an account of himself to God.

Romans 14:11–12

Prayer for Guidance

IN HIS HEART A MAN PLANS HIS COURSE, BUT
THE LORD DETERMINES HIS STEPS.

PROVERBS 16:9

IF GOD listed His top ten most frequently asked questions, "How can I find or know Your will in this matter?" would surely be near the top of that list.

There are many choices we must make in life, and often there are several good options. We know that we need a plan shaped under the guidance of God's Spirit and the truth of His Word, but the steps to that are not always easy or clear. So how do we choose the best—God's best—for us at any given time? How do we find His perfect path and stay out of the briar patches? How do we know that what we're doing or where we're headed is what He would choose for us? How do we find the honey of God's perfect will?

This was our dilemma on the Pastoral Search Committee on which I was serving. People who are very familiar with us and with our needs as a church had presented us with an abundance of wonderful names. They knew these men whose names they had given us as potential candidates, and told us that each one was a man of integrity and giftedness and would be a very good match for our church.

So our committee began to pray fervently, "Oh Lord, how

can we possibly choose? It seems that any one of these candidates would be a good choice, but how do we find Your choice—Your man to lead us into Your future? Clearly, You will have to do the choosing. And please be very, very obvious. We promise to follow."

We would spend the first part of every one of our meetings praying like this for God's leading, and praying for every man whose name was before us, and any potential candidates God would yet send to us. Our entire church was praying. Each committee member had a special prayer team lifting us up as individuals and as a committee.

One day God reminded me that the best way to pray is to pray His own Word to Him. So I pulled together a scriptural prayer for God's guidance and sent it to each committee member. I now realize that this is a prayer capable of leading anyone to God's best for any need in life.

So I share it with you, along with the news that it really works. Or, more accurately, God really works in response to His Word prayed by those committed to obey and follow.

God led us to a man whose name we did not yet have, in the most remarkable, thrilling, miraculous display of guidance any of us on that committee had experienced. From a place of pain, God has taken our church through deep healing under gifted interim pastors—Dr. Tom Correll and then Dr. Dennis Baker. He is now leading us into an exciting future with our new Senior Pastor Tony Silvestri—a man whose heart is tuned to God, His people, and the lost in a way rarely seen. I am convinced that God's kingdom is about to increase, because we prayed—and meant—this prayer, which is my personalized adaptation of Scripture—one of my favorite ways to pray:

Dear Lord,

We have planned many things in our hearts, but we praise you that it is your purpose that prevails. (Proverbs 19:21)

And so we pray (most earnestly), show us your ways, O Lord, teach us your paths; guide us in your truth and teach us, for you are God, our Savior, and our hope is in you all day long. . . . Because you are good and upright, Lord, you have promised to instruct sinners in your ways. You guarantee that you will guide the humble in what is right and teach us your way as we bow before you. . . .

Who, then, are those who fear the Lord? [We are] . . . Therefore, you promise to instruct us in the way chosen for us. Oh Lord, [this is so amazing!] you actually confide in those who fear you. (Psalm 25:4–5, 8–9, 12, 14)

You tell us, "Whether you turn to the right or to the left, your ears will hear a voice behind you saying, 'This is the way; walk in it.'" (Isaiah 30:21)

How wonderful that you, the Holy One, the Lord our God, teach us what is best for us, and direct us in the way we should go! (Isaiah 48:17)

So Lord, we fully commit to you whatever we do, knowing that we will succeed; for we have your assurance that you work out everything for your own ends. (Proverbs 16:3–4)

You say, "I will guide you in the ways of wisdom and lead you along straight paths." (Proverbs 4:11)

We say, "We will follow your ways of wisdom, Lord, and gratefully and joyously walk along your straight paths leading us to the way you have chosen for us. "Thank you! We ask all this in Jesus' precious name, amen.

The LORD is near to all who call on him, to all who call on him in truth. He fulfills the desires of those who fear him; he hears their cry and saves them. The LORD watches over all who love him.

Psalm 145:18–20

This is what the LORD says, he who made the earth, the LORD who formed it and established it—the LORD is his name: "Call to me and I will answer you and tell you great and unsearchable things you do not know."   *Jeremiah 33:2–3*

Forget the former things; do not dwell on the past. See, I am doing a new thing! Do you not perceive it?   *Isaiah 43:18–19*

Thanks be to God, who always leads us in triumphal procession in Christ and through us spreads everywhere the fragrance of the knowledge of him.   *2 Corinthians 2:14*

The Right to Be Right

GOD MADE THEE PERFECT, NOT IMMUTABLE.
JOHN MILTON

I WAS having a discussion with my dentist about the desire to be right when dealing with a difference of opinion. At least as much of a discussion as one can have while reclining in a chair with a mouth full of rubber-gloved activity.

He laughingly commented that he and his wife spend quite a bit of time both being right. To resolve this, he explained, they sometimes take turns. "I get to be right this time, Honey," one of them will announce gleefully.

I'd want to use a turn like that wisely. If I finally got to be right, I wouldn't waste it. I'd want to turn it to best advantage!

However, this "fair play system" doesn't work in our relationship with God. Whether we chafe under, or rest in this, the fact remains, God is always right. He doesn't have a need to be right in order to feel better about Himself, or to "win"—He just is right! That's the way it is with Perfection—One Who doesn't just know the truth, but actually *is* the Truth.

So we simply don't have the option of taking turns at the controls with Him. And when we try, it never works to our advantage. When I say, either through words or actions, "It's my turn—I'll do it my way—have it my way," it leads to a wrong turn every time.

Lord,
You have never heard me pray,
"My will be done."
Yet every time I fail to say,
"Thy will be done,"
You hear my silent stubborn cry
And leave me to some dead-end try.
Oh, kind and patient Loving One.
I'm wiser now, "Thy will be done!"

As for God, his way is perfect; the word of the Lord is flawless.
He is a shield for all who take refuge in him.   Psalm 18:30

All a man's ways seem right to him, but the Lord weighs the
heart.   Proverbs 21:2

Who can discern his [her] errors? Forgive my hidden faults.
                                                    Psalm 19:12

"I will teach you the way that is good and right."   1 Samuel
12:23

Do not conform any longer to the pattern of this world, but be
transformed by the renewing of your mind. Then you will be
able to test and approve what God's will is—his good, pleasing
and perfect will.   Romans 12:2

Options Aren't Optional Anymore

MULTITUDES, MULTITUDES IN THE VALLEY OF
DECISION!   JOEL 3:14

I JUST figured out what's wrong with me these days. (Well, one of the things, anyway.) I think I'm being "optioned to death." The options of abundance are everywhere. This is not only embarrassing, it's baffling and overwhelming. Simply buying orange juice in the morning has been known to use up my entire day's allotment of decision-making ability.

After deciding not to simply buy an orange from the produce department—fatally flawed decision—I finally choose to go to the refrigerated section, rather than the frozen food case, or the shelf. Now, do I want fresh-squeezed, reconstituted, or will ten percent genuine juice suffice? Name brand or store brand? From Florida or California oranges? In a carton, plastic container, or glass? Institutional, gallon, half gallon, or pint size? No pulp, low pulp, or lotsa pulp? Added calcium, vitamin D, or iron? Straight O. J. or mixed with tangerine, mango, or papaya juice? Do I want to pay for this with cash, check, ATM, or credit card? And by the way, would I like this bagged in paper or plastic?

I've barely swallowed my juice and I'm already ready for bed. I was going to get some toothpaste, but I think I saw a woman having a nervous breakdown in that aisle.

Even something as spiritual as getting a Bible has become a vale of agonizing decision-making. Should I get a translation or a paraphrase, and which one of the umpteen versions? (Won't people judge me by my version?) A Study Bible? Which one?

Perhaps a Devotional Bible. Oh Lord, help me here! Even knowing my gender isn't enough anymore. If I'm married am I required to get the Couple's Devotional Bible instead of just the Women's? No, I'm a mom so maybe I should get that one. But I'm a little compulsive, so perhaps the one for addicts would be best? And another thing, is it even legal for a woman to read a Men's Devotional Bible, or an adult to read a Student Bible?

But I still don't have my Bible. More choices to be made. Do I want a little pocket size with a fold-over snap cover, a regular size, or an impressive ten-pounder? Leather bound, hardback, or paperback? (What exactly is bonded leather, anyway?) With concordance and maps, or not? Jesus' words highlighted? I'm required to choose a color now? Do I want pink? Isn't black holier? My name imprinted on it? What do you mean, do I want a cross, a fish, or a butterfly with that? Aren't you going to ask if I want take-out or delivery?

What? You think I should consider a Computer Bible? That would be a round Bible with a hole in the center and I don't have to make a color choice? I'll have the daily option (oh no, not that!) of every known translation at once, plus full concordance, word and subject search tools, commentaries, and devotions by my favorite author? Greek? Do I want a Sepwhoagint? Does aspirin come with that?

It's a different world these days. Both better and worse. More exciting, but also more confusing. It's a world that forces us to think and choose constantly. To decide what we want, what God would want for us, and why and when, or else be forever re-deciding. We could easily starve to death while reading the menu in a world like this.

But it's also a world that doesn't afford much time for thinking and choosing. It turns out that we're required to choose even that—to make the all-important choice that sets aside time to study and meditate on God's Word in order to learn God's good will for us. But it's time well spent, for it saves us so much agonizing. Understanding and agreeing with the commands and values of God's Word today removes the need to make repeated on-the-spot choices later, regarding whether to do or not to do what's right.

In life's difficult "disputable matters" we lean on our all-important prior decision to follow the leading of God's Spirit in all things, and to honor one another in love.

But there are still all those daily decisions that are not choices between what is right or wrong, but are simply the options of life. I believe that God wants us to know who He has designed us to be, and to gratefully choose what honors that created uniqueness without being self-indulgent and without shortchanging someone else. His Spirit of wisdom sorts through our deep pile of wants and finds our genuine needs. For although our heavenly Father seems to enjoy blessing us by granting us many of our wants, His promise is to meet all of our needs.

And finally, deciding not to waste time or energy struggling over the small stuff, and choosing to live in tune with God's best, leaving the rest, has a way of taking the sting out of options and putting back the sweet joy of freedom in Christ.

> *You, my brothers [and sisters], were called to be free. But do not use your freedom to indulge the sinful nature; rather, serve one another in love.*   Galatians 5:13

> *Let us choose what is right; let us determine among ourselves what is good.*   Job 34:4 NRSV

Do not forsake wisdom, and she will protect you; love her and she will watch over you.   *Proverbs 4:6*

Are there those who respect the Lord? He will point them to the best way.   *Psalm 25:12 NCV*

B✿dy Talk

WE'RE WAITING THE ARRIVAL OF THE SAVIOR,
THE MASTER, JESUS CHRIST, WHO WILL
TRANSFORM OUR EARTHY BODIES INTO GLORI-
OUS BODIES LIKE HIS OWN. HE'LL MAKE US
BEAUTIFUL AND WHOLE.

PHILIPPIANS 3:21 THE MESSAGE

I JUST love it when earnest, well-meaning people say things like, "You need to tune in to your body." I find this to be totally unnecessary advice. My body talks constantly whether I tune in or not. In fact, the radio doesn't even have to be plugged in. It's getting more and more like that all-news radio station that bandies about the slogan; "All talk, all the time!"

It's amazing how much trouble a body can give, given enough time. Morning, noon, and night it's, "Don't you have another hand you can use?"

"Just because I'm your foot doesn't mean you can walk all over me like that!"

"You're trying to tell me I actually digested this before . . . and liked it?"

"I'm serious here, give me a break or I'll give you one!"

Talk, talk, talk. How about a little music for a change?

As the thorns and thistles of our failing bodies press in on us, we could use a good dose of God's truth and hope. We need to be reminded that God values us, body and soul. Jesus came to save and redeem us from the curse of sin, body and soul. He actually chose to make our bodies the dwelling place of His Spirit.

Sometimes I wonder if it would have been possible for God to save our souls without having to save our bodies. Couldn't He just toss these spoiled human forms aside when we die and give us something completely different to live in for eternity? If this were possible, it might have saved Jesus the agony of having to enter into human skin with all the terrible pain and suffering He took on.

But whether or not He could have done this, He didn't. He didn't take any shortcuts to salvation. Clearly, God values what He creates. And when God saves, He "saves to the uttermost."

It constantly amazes me to realize that Jesus didn't come into this world just as a baby; He came first as an embryo and then a fetus. This Magnificent One—who forever fills the universes and beyond with His unimaginable vastness, His limitless glorious immensity—somehow squeezed Himself tight, and for nine long months huddled within the cramped belly of a woman. Waiting. And being jostled and jolted along on the back of a donkey all the way to Bethlehem.

Finally, He painfully squeezed through a narrow birth canal to face a mother's arms, yes. But also barnyard smells—hunger— thirst—cold—unbelief—temptations—ingratitude—misunder-standing—bruises—beatings—mocking—thorns—and death on a cruel cross, suspended on our spikes.

I am as amazed that He *could* do this, as I am that He *would* do it. Love far beyond comprehension . . . but thankfully not beyond reach.

The Bible tells us that the kind of body that rose from the grave when Jesus conquered death after three days, is the same kind of body we will one day wear. His body will bear forever the scars of love's sacrifice, but with none of the pain, limitations, sickness, brokenness, or decay. Our inheritance in Christ is to be a glorious body whose only "talk" is praise and joy. A body fit to walk into the presence of a holy God and thank Him. A body as God designed it to be, dancing the dance of the redeemed and never getting tired.

Sounds like somebody tuned my station to heaven's music. Let's dance!

So we're not giving up. How could we! Even though on the outside it often looks like things are falling apart on us, on the inside, where God is making new life, not a day goes by without his unfolding grace. These hard times are small potatoes compared to the coming good times, the lavish celebration prepared for us. There's far more here than meets the eye. The things we see now are here today, gone tomorrow. But the things we can't see now will last forever.

For instance, we know that when these bodies of ours are taken down like tents and folded away, they will be replaced by resurrection bodies in heaven—God-made, not handmade—and we'll never have to relocate our "tents" again. Sometimes we can hardly wait to move—and so we cry out in frustration. Compared to what's coming, living conditions around here seem like a stopover in an unfurnished shack, and we're tired of it! We've been given a glimpse of the real thing, our true home, our resurrection bodies! The Spirit of God whets our appetite by giving us a taste of what's ahead. He puts a little of heaven in our hearts so that we'll never settle for less.

That's why we live with such good cheer. You won't see us drooping our heads or dragging our feet! Cramped conditions here don't get us down. They only remind us of the spacious living conditions ahead. It's what we trust in but don't yet see that keeps us going. 2 Corinthians 4:16—5:7 *The Message*

Oh my soul, bless Yahweh. From head to toe, I'll bless his holy name! Oh my soul, bless Yahweh, don't forget a single blessing!

> *He forgives your sins—every one.*
> *He heals your diseases—every one.*
> *He redeems you from hell—saves your life!*
> *He crowns you with love and mercy—a paradise crown.*
> *He wraps you in goodness—beauty eternal.*
> *He renews your youth—you're always young in his presence.*

Psalm 103:1–5 The Message

Truth in the Midst of Humor

WHEN TRUTH'S ARROW IS SHOT FROM THE
BOW OF LAUGHTER IT FINDS AN OPEN TARGET.

SL

I JUST finished serving on my church's pastoral search committee, and I worked with an amazing mixture of diverse and thoroughly delightful people. Guided by an excellent and widely used pastoral search process manual (and by the man who wrote it, Dr. Dennis Baker, who also happened to be our interim pastor), we prayed and worked hard to find and confirm God's choice for our senior pastor.

People had reason to doubt our diligence as a committee, however. We enjoyed so much laughter throughout the process that anyone who happened to be standing near the office where we met weekly, might have thought we were having way too much fun to be truly accomplishing anything. But with God's help we accomplished a great deal.

Our church membership cast a one-hundred-percent "yes" vote for the candidate we were thrilled to present through God's unmistakable leading. And then our job as a committee was finished. Just like that, all our search activity stopped, and the constant flurry of communication ended.

Take e-mail, for instance. During the six months we met, so much e-mail activity went on that some of us had to upgrade our computers just to handle it all. As a result, certain committee members developed a "problem" when it came to a screeching halt. Last week we received this e-mail from one member:

Hello. My name is Suzanne . . .

And I'm an e-mail-aholic. I haven't always had this problem.

It started a little over six months ago when I began working on a project that required some e-mail capabilities. It's only a little e-mail, I thought. A little e-mail never hurt anybody, right?

But gradually the project got more intense, and so did the e-mail. It's okay, I thought, I can control it.

Eventually I found myself checking my e-mail first thing in the morning, even before I had breakfast. And again at lunchtime. And it was the last thing I would do before I went to bed every night. Even then, I didn't think I had a problem. I can stop anytime I want, I thought.

The trouble was, I kept getting so many e-mails—sometimes fifteen or sixteen in a single day. I can see now how addictive it was, but I didn't see it then. And now it's too late.

I can admit it now—I'M HOOKED! Sorry . . . sorry. Didn't mean to shout. Sigh.

Well, the project has ended now, so I'm not getting any more e-mail. Oh sure, there's the e-mail from places like Amazon.com, but it's just not the same.

Yesterday . . . yesterday I didn't get one single e-mail. Not one! I kept checking and checking, but nothing! NOTHING! Finally I couldn't take it anymore—I just HAD to send one! I can't go through another day without e-mail. I NEED E-MAIL!

Please, please. IS THERE NO ONE WHO CAN

HELP ME? Gasp, choke. Okay, okay. I'm okay now.
Sorry . . . sorry.

Thanks. I feel better. Feel free to reply.

I roared with laughter, missing afresh those regular meetings
and interactions with dear brothers and sisters. And, of course, I fed
her an immediate e-mail message. Everyone on the committee did.
(And some of the replies were almost as funny as the original.)

I find it particularly delightful when God lets me laugh and
learn at the same time, which is what happened when I received
Suzanne's desperate e-mail plea. I laughed hard at the humor
and was hit hard by the truth hidden in this amusing example
of something that isn't amusing at all when it's a "sin" problem
rather than an e-mail problem.

What is it that we thought we could control that now has
control of us? Is it time for some knee-mail saying, "Help, Lord"?
He's always on line. His Server never fails to deliver the message
of truth and freedom we so desperately need.

*Jesus replied, "I tell you the truth, everyone who sins is a slave
to sin. Now a slave has no permanent place in the family, but a
son belongs to it forever. So if the Son sets you free, you will be
free indeed. . . .*

*"If you hold to my teaching, you are really my disciples.
Then you will know the truth, and the truth will set you free."*

John 8:34–36, 31–32

What Does It Taste Like?

THE whispered question came at the most silent, reverent moment of the communion service—while we were partaking of the elements. The little girl a few seats down from me didn't ask to have a piece of the bread, or one of the small cups of juice—apparently it had been explained to her that she was still too young to understand. But that hadn't stopped her curiosity.

"Daddy," she whispered urgently, eager eyes searching his face as he swallowed, "what does it taste like? Is it good?"

Not wanting to disturb others, her father quieted her with a gentle hand and a smile. But my heart rushed to answer her.

"What does it taste like? Oh, precious child, it's the flavor of love—bittersweet, costly love. It tastes like life, and hope, and joy."

"Is it good? It's the best thing I have ever tasted, or ever will taste. But it's not my tongue that knows this, little one. It's my heart and spirit that savor heaven's sweetest honey, dripping from life's sharpest thorn. You can partake of it, too. One day very soon."

Jesus said, "Let the little children come to me, and do not hinder them, for the kingdom of heaven belongs to such as these."

Matthew 19:14

Taste and see that the LORD *is good; blessed is the man [woman or child] who takes refuge in him.*   Psalm 34:8

With honey from the rock I would satisfy you.   Psalm 81:16

How sweet are your words to my taste, sweeter than honey to my mouth!   Psalm 119:103

Heaven's Sweetest Gift

THANKS BE TO GOD FOR HIS INDESCRIBABLE
GIFT!   2 CORINTHIANS 9:15

Deity in a diaper,
Conqueror in a cradle,
Wisdom in a workshop,
Truth in a temple;
Righteousness in a robe,
Salvation in sandals,
Compassion on a cross,
Triumph in a tomb,
Love in a look,
Life in such love!

The free gift of God is eternal life in Jesus Christ our Lord.
Romans 6:23 TLB

Long ago, even before he made the world, God chose us to be his very own, through what Christ would do for us; he decided then to make us holy in his eyes, without a single fault—we who stand before him covered with his love. His unchanging plan has always been to adopt us into His own family by sending Jesus Christ to die for us. And he did this because he wanted to!

Now all praise to God for his wonderful kindness to us and his favor that he has poured out upon us, because we belong to his dearly loved Son. So overflowing is his kindness toward us that he took away all our sins through the blood of his Son, by whom we are saved; and he has showered down upon us the richness of his grace—for how well he understands us and knows what is best for us at all times.

God has told us his secret reason for sending Christ, a plan he decided on in mercy long ago; and this was his purpose: that when the time is ripe he will gather us all together from wherever we are—in heaven or on earth—to be with him in Christ forever. Moreover, because of what Christ has done, we have become gifts to God that he delights in. . . . God's purpose in this was that we should praise God and give glory to him for doing these mighty things for us.   Ephesians 1:4–12 TLB

How Did *He* Get In Here?

COULD IT BE THAT DISUNITY IS THE REASON
WHY WE ARE NOT WINNING THE WORLD TO
CHRIST?   SELWYN HUGHES

YOUR ENEMY THE DEVIL PROWLS AROUND
LIKE A ROARING LION LOOKING FOR SOMEONE
TO DEVOUR. RESIST HIM, STANDING FIRM IN
THE FAITH. . . .   PETER, 1 PETER 5:8

RECENTLY it dawned on me that the devil goes to church. Oh, he can never become a member. But he's a regular attender. And he wreaks a lot of havoc—wounds a lot of people.

Somehow, he has managed to find a way to ambush God's people, attacking from within that very place where we should all be the safest. The place where we're required to be open and vulnerable in order to be the honest, growing, transparent people of God. The place that must be a haven for those seeking a place to admit they are lost and needy. The place where masks and walls and shut doors don't belong, yet are too often needed.

One wonders, *How does God's enemy manage to get into God's house?*

Jesus said that an intruder cannot ransack a house guarded by a strong man unless he first ties up the strong man (Matthew 12:29). God's enemy has no power to bind up the Strong Man, Jesus, who guards His own house of worship. The Evil One has no power equal to our mighty Lord and Savior!

So how does he get in? How does he find access to this sweetest place on earth—this place that dares to join the heavenly hosts in praising and honoring God in open joy?

Recently a friend and I were talking—grieving really—over how many leaders in the Christian community have been deluded and sidetracked by the enemy and, in falling, have hurt so many others. We lamented over the number of precious brothers and sisters who are caving in to doubts and disillusionment, or dropping away and leaving, wounded and broken. Some stay, lashing out at others in their pain, damaging more people. This friend really knows, for she is a Christian counselor who has worked with hundreds who have been ravaged in the explosions and battlegrounds within our churches.

My friend may have been surprised by what I said next because it didn't seem to logically follow what we were talking about.

"You know," I said, "if God granted me the power to give just one special gift to Christians, I know what I'd give. It would be the gift of seeing, and being strengthened in our weak areas. We need to be able to look honestly at what we withhold, what we deny, and on whom we rely. If only we could allow God's light of truth to shine on our deepest unmet and unacknowledged needs. What a great gift it would be to finally confess those ways in which we're trying to meet our needs outside of God's provision."

She quickly added, "And being able to recognize our strengths gone out of control."

"Yes," I agreed. "I see these as the enemy's entry points into our lives—the places where he sneaks in to mess us up and uses us to mess up and hurt others. I need to write about these things someday. We need to stop the carnage."

God's enemy doesn't set out to destroy the buildings of worship; he goes after the people who worship. After all, the church is made up of God's children. And by getting to the children, he gets to the Father.

When we allow the enemy entry into our lives we become "carriers." We carry him into our churches and let him operate through our words and actions. Certainly we don't intend to do this! Often we don't even know we are doing it. Peter just thought he was being lovingly protective of his Lord when he protested that he should never be killed. Peter didn't know that Satan was speaking with his mouth until Jesus rebuked him (Matthew 16:21–23).

But the enemy is so very clever in how he operates. Even when he has been successful at tying us up in some area, we still feel free, because he is careful never to bind and gag our mouth. Why would he, when he can use it for his destructive activity?

Just a few "judgment calls" voiced. A few pointed words aimed. A confidence broken. A story told, minus a few facts. An opposing opinion that finds several interested ears. Innuendo planted. Anger spilling out. Just a small flaming arrow here and there.

Or he gets us wrapped up in the idea that one tiny wrong choice doesn't count. Just some small behavior outside God's will. Just a little carelessness with God's guidelines for holy living. The beginning of a little flirtation. A power play. A slight infraction of Jesus' law of love. Just a small hand-grenade in the fellowship of believers.

When God's enemy manages to get inside our churches to create havoc and destruction, he manages to discredit Christ. The world looks and laughs, "Jesus saves? Good. I hope He saves me from that!" And they walk away shaking their heads.

The enemy has accomplished his mission. The blind and the lost have once again missed seeing their Savior. They walked away from the One who died to save them from the clutches of this vicious, clever enemy whose mayhem they mock—the One who loves them so deeply.

And the church is left hurting, divided, defeated, and ineffective. We're not only failing to spread the Good News, we seem to be running the presses day and night cranking out the bad news. Mission accomplished.

Are we willing to slam the door on this enemy? Are you and I willing to deal with this prowling lion's entry points into our own lives? Are we willing to stop pointing at other offenders—even the people who have hurt us the most—and begin looking long and hard at our own unprotected entry points, dealing with these areas before God?

When we do that, we will be able to pray with discerning love and wisdom for our offending brothers and sisters. They are not the enemy. Those who have hurt us are hurting. All of us are under attack by our common enemy.

Yet we can all be under the protection of our common, and yet uncommon, Savior! How sweet it is when we let Him save us from the Evil One's tricks and traps. How sweet when the world looks and says, "Behold how they love one another! I want a taste of that!"

This will happen when we get honest before God with ourselves and with others.

When we go before Him in humility and confession—

When we respond to Him in open trusting obedience—

When we challenge one another with the truth spoken in love—

When we bring God's grace and abundance into one another's lives—

When we begin sharing the ripening fruit of the Holy Spirit in joyous thanksgiving.

Then the landscape of our churches will begin to flow with the milk and honey of God's Promised Land instead of the blood of those wounded within our own walls.

What causes fights and quarrels among you? Don't they come from your desires that battle within you? You want something but don't get it. You kill and covet, but you cannot have what you want. You quarrel and fight. You do not have, because you do not ask God. When you ask, you do not receive, because you ask with wrong motives, that you may spend what you get on your pleasures.

Submit yourselves, then, to God. Resist the devil, and he will flee from you. Come near to God and he will come near to you. Wash your hands, you sinners, and purify your hearts, you double-minded.　　　　　　　　　　　　　　　　James 4:1–3, 7–8

The entire Law is summed up in a single command: "Love your neighbor as yourself." If you keep on biting and devouring each other, watch out or you will be destroyed by each other.

So I say, live by the Spirit, and you will not gratify the desires of the sinful nature.

But the fruit of the Spirit is love, joy, peace, patience, kindness, goodness, faithfulness, gentleness and self-control. Against such things there is no law. Those who belong to Christ Jesus have crucified the sinful nature with its passions and desires. Since we live by the Spirit, let us keep in step with the Spirit. Let us not become conceited, provoking and envying each other.

Galatians 5:14–16, 22–26

The Hedge Trimmer

A WORD OUT OF YOUR MOUTH MAY SEEM OF
NO ACCOUNT, BUT IT CAN ACCOMPLISH NEAR-
LY ANYTHING—OR DESTROY IT!
JAMES, JAMES 3:5 THE MESSAGE

LIFE is flawed and difficult enough. But when people take it upon themselves to point out flaws and to criticize, life gets harder. We may find ourselves wanting to turn and "cut them down to size" in return.

Some time ago, I came across a story told by Robert Russell about his pastor friend whose church had doubled in size in just one year under his leadership. Nevertheless, he regularly received critical anonymous letters from someone who signed each note, "The Thorn." Attached to the first note was an explanation: since the apostle Paul had a thorn in the flesh, the writer thought the preacher should have one too, thus the notes saying things the minister didn't want to hear.

Robert said his friend wanted to find out who "The Thorn" was and send an anonymous letter signed, "The Hedge Trimmer."

I appreciate both the humor and the desire. Who hasn't wanted to go to work with a hedge trimmer at times?

But is our hedge trimmer, God's hedge trimmer? Are our ways, God's ways? Do I seek to deal with irritating people and circumstances in the same way that Jesus did?

Jesus had plenty of opportunities to practice hedge-trimming because He had a lot of "thorns" in His life. The Pharisees regularly went out of their way to needle and harass Him. But these religious leaders didn't bother with anonymous notes; they attacked in public. After plotting behind synagogue doors they would catch Jesus, often in some crowded situation, and pose questions they thought would stymie and expose Him. They set clever traps to discredit Him. They spread rumors and lies. They even paid a friend to betray Him.

How did Jesus handle all this? Sometimes He asked pointed questions in return. Sometimes He met them head on. Sometimes He avoided them. Sometimes He exposed their evil intent with stories. Sometimes He even called them names. But where He found any openness at all, He drew them toward the light. He never gave up. But in the end, He allowed them to catch Him in their evil plot so that He could nail evil to the cross.

In every response, Jesus was guided by the Spirit and did only what the Father wanted Him to do. In every experience, His Father guided Him to do and say exactly what was right for that particular person and situation. I have to wonder, do I even care, sometimes, what the Father wants when I'm irritated and want to lash out?

In every situation, Jesus spoke the truth and lived the truth. But He wasn't always polite according to our standards. Politeness is sometimes the coward's cover for being unwilling to speak the truth in love.

In every situation, He loved the person while hating and exposing the sin that was warping and destroying the person. Redemptive love was always available, though it was not always welcomed or received.

And the final irony is that He knew He was responding to irritating, maddening, vicious people for whom He was about to lay down His life.

Can my hedge trimmer stand up to that?

If you suffer for doing good and you endure it, this is commendable before God. To this you were called, because Christ suffered for you, leaving you an example, that you should follow in his steps.

"He committed no sin, and no deceit was found in his mouth."

When they hurled their insults at him, he did not retaliate; when he suffered, he made no threats. Instead, he entrusted himself to him who judges justly. He himself bore our sins in his body on the tree, so that we might die to sins and live for righteousness: by his wounds you have been healed.   1 Peter 2:20–24

This is how we know what love is: Jesus Christ laid down his life for us. And we ought to lay down our lives for our brothers.

Dear children, let us not love with words or tongue but with actions and in truth.   1 John 3:16, 18

Salted Grace Talk

LET YOUR CONVERSATION BE ALWAYS FULL OF
GRACE, SEASONED WITH SALT, SO THAT YOU
MAY KNOW HOW TO ANSWER EVERYONE.
                    PAUL, COLOSSIANS 4:6

ASK anyone who's been placed on a salt-restricted diet how eager she is for a bowl of popcorn. Ask if the wonderful scents wafting from a warm plate of food still deliver a taste as good as their smell promises.

A few simple grains of salt do amazing things to enhance the flavor of our fare. Perfectly seasoned foods cause our taste buds to rise up and cheer. While too much salt ruins a thing, the absence of salt can make chewing a chore, taking much of the appeal out of the life-sustaining act of eating.

Have you ever tried to share the life-giving Gospel with someone who is starving spiritually and found that it wasn't being eagerly swallowed—or that they didn't come back for more? Ever offered words of wisdom to a friend or family member desperately in need and find them seemingly disinterested—even turned off? Ever had someone ask for your input and then ignore it?

We can feel frustrated or even angry because, after all, shouldn't the "plain truth" be enough? What more can they want?

We need to go to God's spice rack, for our words must be properly seasoned with wisdom and grace. Generous sprinklings of kindness, gentleness, good humor, and humility make words easier to swallow. And, face it, we need a little salt.

God's salt makes our conversation interesting, provocative, lively. No clichés or formulas. No tasteless cafeteria conversation. Salt means we think and pray before and while we speak, so that our words are fresh and mouth-watering. Salt means we listen carefully to the whisper of God's Spirit because He knows the unique needs and taste preferences of the person to whom we're speaking. God's salt brings out the full flavor of grace . . . and it tastes a lot like love in action.

> *Say only what helps, each word a gift.*
> *Ephesians 4:29 The Message*

> *Taste and see that the LORD is good.*   *Psalm 34:8*

> *Grow up in your salvation, now that you have tasted that the Lord is good.*   *1 Peter 2:2–3*

Grace Goes the Distance

GRACE IS HEAVEN'S PERSONAL PRONOUN AND
MERCY'S VERB.   SL

I slammed the door.
Grace tiptoed in and smiled.

I fell hard.
Grace stretched out a hand.

I lectured myself.
Grace whispered love.

I pushed away.
Grace waited and prayed.

I dropped to my knees.
Grace welcomed me home.

I walked on in joy.
Grace blazed the trail.

I looked behind.
Grace had a following.

A sight to take your breath away! Grand processions of people telling all the good things of God! Romans 10:15 The Message

In the Messiah, in Christ, God leads us from place to place in one perpetual victory parade. Through us, he brings knowledge of Christ. 2 Corinthians 2:14 The Message

Every detail works to your advantage and to God's glory: more and more grace, more and more people, more and more praise! 2 Corinthians 4:15 The Message

From the fullness of his grace we have all received one blessing after another. John 1:16

The grace of Christ is the only good ground for life. Hebrews 13:9 The Message

What God Hears

A FRIEND told me the other day that he was walking down the aisle of a church as everyone stood singing and actually saw an older man sitting down with his fingers stuck into his ears. Most people only do that on the inside when they don't like the music.

I wonder if God sometimes "has His fingers in His ears" when we sing? While we hear only the sounds coming from our collective mouths, He hears our songs over the din of critical attitudes and objections coming from within so many hearts about the style of music or some other discontent. I wonder how He feels about this lovely, lyrical gift—a gift He generously gave so that we would have some harmonious, joyful way to honor and lift Him up—being contaminated with discord and nasty disagreement?

Clever, clever enemy, who dares to take songs intended as the praise due the Almighty and hold them on the lathe of people's personal preference until they become sharp enough to pierce the heart of God. Foolish, foolish people, who let—even help—the enemy turn God's praise into a cacophony in His ears with pointed opinions devoid of grace. He says that without love we are like clanging symbols. And we thought it was the music.

Perhaps Satan gets away with creating such ugly dissonance because we forget why God gave us the gift of music and song.

We begin to think it is so that we can build our spiritual memories around it and press the replay button. So that we can know all the words and what comes next and slip into cozy familiarity in the "church club."

In his book *The Joyful Christian*, C. S. Lewis commented that it seemed to him that "we often, almost sulkily, reject the good that God offers us because, at that moment, we expected some other good." He included our "religious experience" in his list saying, "we are always harking back to some occasion which seemed to us to reach perfection, setting that up as the norm, and depreciating all other occasions by comparison." He had begun to suspect that these experiences are often "full of their own new blessing, if only we would lay ourselves open to it." Then he made this sad statement: "God shows us a new facet of the glory, and we refuse to look at it because we're still looking for the old one."

Music is the voice God gave our souls to release our growing wonder, joy, and gratitude over who He is, what He has done, and what He is now doing for us. How can we not sing a new song? He is ever a discovery—ever the same, yet ever new. Our musical worship is meant to be beautiful, good, fresh, and alive because it is to reflect Him. And it is intended to make His heart glad. It is intended to create a throne for Him to sit on among us. True, it often comforts, thrills, and reminds us of His goodness and care. But, really, it is all about Him, not at all about us.

Our musical worship is also meant to reveal (declare and proclaim) His beauty and love to a lost world. I have a friend who, before she came to know Jesus, was invited to attend our Tuesday morning women's Bible study. She told me later that when she walked into that room and saw and heard all of us standing there singing our songs of praise before our study began, she was transfixed. She said, "Wow, God. You must really be someone special. All these women took time out of their busy morning to come here and sing to You like this!" She got the message, and God got the glory that time. Because we were focusing on singing to Him.

It must be a particularly terrible sound to God when we mindlessly sing words of truth, praise, and commitment while our thoughts and hearts are elsewhere. In the book by the prophet Isaiah, we read these words of the Lord: "These people come near to me with their mouth and honor me with their lips, but their hearts are far from me" (29:13). Surely we don't want to be guilty of this.

My friend Ben West was invited to give a devotional talk to his church choir on the subject of worship. To illustrate the difference between mechanical and spiritual worship, he told about an experience he'd had a couple of weeks before his dear wife, Sharon, had died of cancer.

While massaging her back he began to think about what a precious treasure she was to him and how much he loved her. Seconds after he thought that, she said, "I feel so loved when you rub me like that!"

"Somehow," he told the choir through his tears, "my massage changed when I put my heart into it, and she immediately sensed it. Our musical message, too, will change when we put our hearts into it. God wants to be able to say, 'I feel so loved when you sing like that!'"

Oh, let's love God in our singing! And let's love one another as we sing by offering and participating in a variety of ways to express our love and joy in Him. Let's be tender and considerate of one another, proving that we are related to Christ. And when we can't quite enjoy all the "variety," we can at least look around and delight in seeing others worship in a way that is different from our way, preferring one another above ourselves. We can always use the time to pray that God will be honored in all things, and that all of His children will be blessed in worshiping Him.

Offering up our personal opinions, pet peeves, and musical preferences so that all can know and rejoice in Him is our "sacrifice of praise." This is harmony that begins in hearts and ends in glad voices joined in eternal harmonious praise. What a sweet sound to His ears!

God is here—let's celebrate! With song and with dance, with stringed instruments and brass, with cymbals and drums, let us express exuberant joy in God's presence. Let us celebrate with the old songs of praise. Let us also create new songs that portray the eternal love of our God.

Psalm 33:1–3 Psalms Now, Leslie F. Brandt

Praise the LORD. Sing to the LORD a new song, his praise in the assembly of the saints.   *Psalm 149:1*

"A time is coming and has now come when the true worshipers will worship the Father in spirit and truth, for they are the kind of worshipers the Father seeks. God is spirit, and his worshipers must worship in spirit and in truth."   John 4:23–24

Worship the LORD with gladness; come before him with joyful songs. Know that the LORD is God. It is he who made us, and we are his; we are his people, the sheep of his pasture. Enter his gates with thanksgiving and his courts with praise; give thanks to him and praise his name.   Psalm 100:2–4

Ascribe to the LORD, *O families of nations, ascribe to the* LORD *glory and strength, ascribe to the* LORD *the glory due his name. Bring an offering and come before him; worship the* LORD *in the splendor of his holiness.*   1 Chronicles 16:28–29

I will sing to the LORD *all my life; I will sing praise to my God as long as I live. May my meditation be pleasing to him, as I rejoice in the* LORD.   Psalm 104:33–34

The Thorn

AND THEY CLOTHED HIM WITH PURPLE; AND
THEY TWISTED A CROWN OF THORNS, PUT IT
ON HIS HEAD, AND BEGAN TO SALUTE HIM,
"HAIL, KING OF THE JEWS!"
                              MARK 15:17–18 NKJV

Once I heard a sound of sweetness,
As it cleft the morning air,
Sounding in its blest completeness,
Like a tender pleading prayer;
And I sought to find the singer,
Whence the wondrous song was borne;
And I found a bird, sore wounded,
Pinioned by a cruel thorn.
I have seen a soul in sadness,
While its wings with pain were furl'ed,
Giving hope, and cheer and gladness
That should bless a weeping world;
And I knew that life of sweetness,
Was of pain and sorrow borne,
And a stricken soul was singing,
With its heart against a thorn
Ye are told of One Who loved you,
Of a Saviour crucified,
Ye are told of nails that pinioned,

And a spear that pierced His side;
Ye are told of cruel scourging,
Of a Saviour bearing scorn,
And He died for your salvation,
With His brow against a thorn.
Ye "are not above the Master."
Will you breathe a sweet refrain?
And His grace will be sufficient,
When your heart is pierced with pain.
Will you live to bless His loved ones,
Tho' your life be bruised and torn,
Like the bird that sang so sweetly,
With its heart against a thorn?

    Author Unknown
    from *Streams in the Desert,*
    Mrs. Charles E. Cowman

So then, those who suffer according to God's will should commit
themselves to their faithful Creator and continue to do good. . . .
*   And the God of all grace, who called you to his eternal*
glory in Christ, after you have suffered a little while, will himself
restore you and make you strong, firm and steadfast. To him be
the power for ever and ever. Amen.   1 Peter 4:19; 5:10–11

Grappling with the Pain of 9-11

AWAY FROM ME, ALL YOU WHO DO EVIL, FOR
THE LORD HAS HEARD MY WEEPING.
                                        PSALM 6:8

"WHY do you think God permitted this Trade Center trag-edy, Mom? Why didn't He prevent such a terrible thing?" my son asked.

"If only I knew," I said after a long pause. "This is so heart-breaking, and so difficult to understand. The depth and reach of the pain is almost unimaginable. But this has always been the big question, hasn't it? 'If God is so powerful, why does He allow sin and evil to run rampant? Why do good people suffer?'"

I told my son that while I certainly don't understand all the reasons evil is allowed its reign of terror in this world, I do know it doesn't mean that God is powerless. Then I was almost surprised to hear myself suggest that such tragedies reveal more about the nature of sin, and ultimately the nature of God's love, than they do about His power.

God's intention for us is always for good. He hates sin and death even more than we do. It breaks His loving heart that humanity invited sin into His perfect world, resulting in days like September 11, 2001. A horror like this, I began to understand, reveals to us that the cancer our rebellion against God brought into this world is so very awful, so pervasive and deadly, that to contain it God would have to do one of three things:

- Remove our free will
- Wipe out the whole world and every sin-tainted thing and person in it
- Do exactly what He is now doing.

Sin can only be "somewhat contained for a while" or "destroyed completely forever."

Those who continue to rebel against God and commit despicable acts perpetuate and escalate evil's terrible reign in our world. Tragedy is here because sinful people are here. Sinful people are here because God's love and grace are here, waiting and yearning for all to turn from deadly, dark evil and come to His light and love.

I can only conclude that if God doesn't rip away our free will, or wipe us out with no recourse—and it's important to realize that the integrity of His amazing love prevents Him from doing either of these things—then He can only do exactly what He is doing. Which is to first give of His own blood to solve our sin problem, and then to continue executing His long-range rescue plan that will one day chain up evil in a bottomless pit and establish a kingdom of righteousness forever. Meanwhile, He allows us time to come to salvation and eternal life in Jesus Christ.

The only possible reason we are still in the midst of this kind of pain is God's willingness to continue to suffer along with us, even after He paid sin's death-price for us. And He makes it clear that He does suffer with us, as His Spirit prays for us with groaning that cannot even be uttered. He waits to give us time to turn to Him and be saved eternally from the midst of it. We are being given time to come and bring others along.

It's important to remember that God already destroyed sin's power over us through His death and resurrection. Soon He will destroy the reality of sin's evil effect throughout creation. When that happens, there will be judgment for everyone who has sided with evil, eternally rejecting His gracious way of escape.

Jesus said to him, "I am the way, the truth, and the life. No one comes to the Father except through me."   *John 14:6 NKJV*

"Whoever comes to me I will never drive away. For my Father's will is that everyone who looks to the Son and believes in him shall have eternal life, and I will raise him up at the last day."
John 6:37, 40

I tell you, now is the time of God's favor, now is the day of salvation.   *2 Corinthians 6:2*

Because God Gave Me Herb

MANY A MAN CLAIMS TO HAVE UNFAILING
LOVE, BUT A FAITHFUL MAN WHO CAN FIND?
PROVERBS 20:6

- My heart found a home outside its own skin.
- I know that faithfulness is a man, not just a word.
- I had a dearly loved friend by my side for thirty-two years.
- I am the mother of three incredibly unique and precious children.
- I know how it feels to share laughter, tears, unspoken thoughts, intimacy, change, struggles, and inside jokes that go way back.
- I've experienced the luxury of being cherished and nourished.
- I know that greeting cards are recyclable, and brown paper bags a superior gift wrap.
- I've learned to respect, and even delight in the differences.
- I have learned that, given enough time and love, tact can be acquired.
- I learned that salsa is breakfast food.
- I discovered that "engineer" is not a profession, but a personality type.

- I know how many miles a full bladder can still go.
- I've come to understand that flowers aren't as important as faithfulness.
- I've learned that God loves a woman very well through a godly man.
- I've shared the challenge to grow and become.
- I am a better, stronger person, even separated from him, than I ever would have been without him.
- I am rich with shared memories.
- I will be eternally grateful.
- Because God gave me Herb, and then took him home before me, part of my heart is already in heaven.

"The LORD gave and the LORD has taken away; may the name of the LORD be praised."   *Job 1:21*

Precious in the sight of the LORD is the death of his saints.   *Psalm 116:15*

Tribute I shared at Herb's Memorial Service on March 3, 1995.

Here We Go Again

I'M thinking I should quit writing books. Either that, or write and ship them directly to press before God has a chance to give me any more life experiences that might make a good addendum.

But it's too late this time, because there was that dangerous time lapse between my submission of this manuscript and the publication date. So I may as well just go ahead and spend a few pages telling you what the last few months offered in the way of raw material. (I rarely get sympathy from anyone, you know. They just smile and say things like, "More grist for the mill!" Thanks so much. It's for this very reason that I love writing so. Who can resist the allure of a life rich with resource trauma?)

I've wondered at the statistical likelihood of having three out of the four women in one family all hospitalized for surgery within a six-week period. I've wondered what the chances are that a woman would have both a son and son-in-law looking for employment while each caring for a wife unable to walk. The chances are apparently very good for this woman.

I didn't see any of this coming. All I saw was December coming. Sure, I knew that our holiday season was going to be a bit more complicated this year since my daughter, in pain and unable to walk again, was scheduled to have another major hip replacement and reconstruction surgery on December 3, this time with bone grafting. Although she would be recovering in a hospital bed at my house, at least we'd be together for the holidays. I reminded myself that when she's healthy, her work keeps her away and exhausted so I don't get to see her as much as I'd like. We would make this work.

But at the end of November, I blacked out while simply sitting and watching television. When it started to happen again a couple of days later, I was hospitalized for observation. Extensive tests turned up nothing, so doctors prescribed a sophisticated little portable heart monitor that I was to wear for a month. They allowed me to go home but said that I couldn't drive at all until this mystery was solved. The hospital staff moved heaven and earth to release me early on the day of Cathy's surgery so that I could make it over to her hospital before she got out of surgery. But getting there wasn't easy.

Picture me wandering around the hospital parking lot in search of my car—which I had not parked and had no idea where it was—in a drizzling cold rain, with no coat, carrying my personal effects in a sack. People looking for a parking space began to follow me in their cars. I repeatedly had to explain that I didn't know where my car was. So embarrassing.

I know you're wondering, *Why isn't someone picking her up?* I had planned to call on my cell phone and arrange a ride closer to the time I'd be ready to leave since I still needed to go to the cardiology department and get hooked up to a portable heart monitor, plus pick up a prescription that I was to start taking. But when I was ready to phone, my cell battery was dead. *Why didn't I just call from a pay phone then?* My wallet had been sent home for safe-keeping, so I had no money or phone card. *How then did I get my prescription?* I didn't. I discovered my wallet missing after standing in line waiting for the prescription to be filled. That's when I also discovered that I still needed to pick up my credit card which was locked up in the hospital safe. *Why was I running around in the rain trying to find my car when I wasn't allowed to drive?* My coat and cell phone charger were inside my car. *Why couldn't I find a ride even when I finally found the car and got my cell phone connected?* No one was home. *What did God do when He saw me fighting back tears and feeling more frustrated and alone than I can ever remember?* He sent a friend who lives in my neighborhood and who is also fighting a disease. When I finally came in out of the rain—after retrieving my credit card and belongings—and returned to the prescription line, there was my friend, waiting in the same line for his own prescription. How like God to send yet another dear wounded one to the rescue. My friend took me home so I could change clothes, and by then, my daughter-in-law Margie was available to take me to Cathy's hospital. When I got there, she had already been returned to her room.

I spent the next nine days bumming rides from gracious friends to and from Cathy's bedside. One Friday night, Cathy went into a pain management crisis when all my usual chauffeurs were at holiday gatherings, so I couldn't find a ride to the hospital to be with my weeping and hysterical daughter. I finally reached a nearby friend who was home recovering from shoulder surgery. With her good arm, she drove me to the hospital, staying to pray and just be there for me while I tried to be there for my daughter through her searing pain. Another wounded one helping a wounded one. A pattern was developing.

That night when we weren't even sure Cathy would live through the pain, I said, "If my monitor doesn't go off tonight, surely there can't be anything wrong with my heart. At least nothing stress induced!"

Several days later, Cathy got to come home. I was trying to take care of her while my daughter-in-law Margie tried to take care of both of us. My heart was playing plenty of strange rhythms, but nothing life-threatening. My son and son-in-law were fighting some kind of flu, while my youngest son, Matt, and his bride, Kelly, were visiting her family in South Africa for the month. But, hey, we were making it. No real complaints.

And then, the day Cathy was first able to get up and crutch her way to the restroom and back to her bed, my heart monitor claimed I needed to go to the emergency room. The cardiologist reading my phoned-in EKG said that I'd just had a short run of "V-tack" and asked if there was anyone who could drive me to the emergency room. Immediately would be good, she said.

Drive? Cathy and I looked at one another and burst out laughing. "No one here allowed behind the wheel," we said.

While I kept saying I felt fine, and they kept talking about sending an ambulance, and my daughter kept dialing her cell phone trying to locate a friend to take me to emergency, God quietly sent Margie through our front door. She just "popped in" to see if we needed anything when she ran to the store. On her heels came Wes, Cathy's husband who wasn't expected for another hour. Wes stayed with Cathy while Margie took me to the emergency room. Jehovah Jireh—God provides!

But now I was hospitalized and hooked up to monitors again—this time for several more days. Friends and family—those who weren't sick and were still in town—tried to divide their time between visiting me and helping care for Cathy in my absence. At least they didn't have to drive me around during that time. Wes was dividing his time between working, interviewing for new jobs (since his contract was about to run out), being Cathy's night nurse, caring for their house and pets, and also caring for my house.

Meantime, I was being subjected to tests and more tests, which continued to show nothing but healthy arteries and a healthy heart. Finally, on Christmas Eve, the surgeon took me into the operating room and ran an unusual test that probed the heart and eventually uncovered what he called a rare electrical problem. Apparently, my heart muscle wasn't getting the signal to contract on occasion, and so it just didn't. Not a good thing if you want to remain conscious.

So, on Christmas Day, of all days, they put in a pacemaker. No roast beef for me! Nothing to eat or drink at all, in fact. But I got to go home the next day. And I didn't have to wander around the parking lot or anything.

When we walked in my front door I discovered the twelve-foot Christmas tree my kids had wrestled into my living room as a surprise. I had asked for just a small one if they had time. There it stood, naked and regal, smelling wonderful. So we wounded and weary ones sat around this towering bare tree and were thankful to just be there and to be together. True, some of us were missing—we always miss Herb so much at Christmas, and my youngest son and his wife were half a world away—but those of us God had spared and brought together could rejoice in the gift of one another. And so, in the midst of it all, we did exactly that.

In the following days, Margie helped us as much as she could. Son Jeff was tied up with resumes and interviews as he had unexpectedly lost his job in the midst of all this. Margie had also been laid off some months earlier or she would have been unavailable to help us. Needless to say, they were in need of a break from all the pressure. So one day after an Alaskan storm dumped snow all the way to the base of our hills, Jeff and Margie took off to enjoy some sledding. And you thought we didn't do such things in San Diego. We do, but apparently we shouldn't.

Later that day we received a call from the same hospital where Cathy had been. Margie was being admitted to a room just down the hall from Cathy's old room with a badly broken ankle. This was *not* the kind of break she needed! Their sled had rammed into a manzanita bush—which, it turns out, has little give, especially when frozen. It took a five-inch steel plate and several screws to put her back together again. The surgeon explained that it was a serious break and that she wouldn't be bearing any weight on her leg for three months. Cathy wept in empathy for what she knew her sister-in-law was facing in immobility, frustration, and pain.

Days later, Margie came home with a cast from her groin to her toes. She lay in bed with her leg elevated, completely helpless. So we wounded ones tried our best to help our wounded helper.

One day, Cathy crutched her way to a chair so that our most recent trauma patient could lay in the hospital bed at my house, her huge cast propped on a mountain of pillows. We were having a family gathering—trying, actually, to celebrate a belated Christmas with the whole family now that the traveling ones and the hospitalized ones were all finally home.

We were talking about how dangerous it was to be a Lenzkes woman these days. Kelly, still in one piece, said she was aware of this and was stepping very, very carefully.

I laughed and said, "But Kelly, if my Mom was right when she used to claim that things come in threes, then . . ."

"Then I just saved you!" Margie announced from the hospital bed with her leg in the air. It was good to laugh together.

Precious times get more precious when they are threatened. When life gets hard, hearts get softer. There seems to be nothing more important than just having one another to embrace, whatever the day, and however unprepared you are. So what if I was in the hospital having surgery on Christmas Day! Christmas happened when we finally gathered together and gave whatever we had to give to one another. It always does. Sweet. Like licking honey off a thorn.

Note to the Reader

The publisher invites you to share your response to the message of this book by writing Discovery House Publishers, Box 3566, Grand Rapids, MI 49501, USA. For information about other Discovery House books, music, or videos, contact us at the same address or call 1-800-653-8333. Find us on the Internet at http://www.dhp.org/ or send e-mail to books@dhp.org.